7,50
70 S

CONTEMPORARY WRITERS

General Editors
MALCOLM BRADBURY
and
CHRISTOPHER BIGSBY

MURIEL S[...]

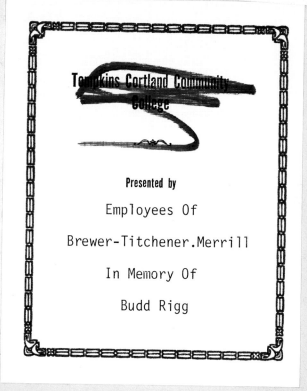

MURIEL
SPARK

ALAN BOLD

METHUEN
LONDON AND NEW YORK

First published in 1986 by
Methuen & Co. Ltd
11 New Fetter Lane, London EC4P 4EE
Published in the USA by
Methuen & Co.
in association with Methuen, Inc.
29 West 35th Street, New York, NY 10001

© 1986 Alan Bold

Typeset by Rowland Phototypesetting Ltd
Printed in Great Britain by
Richard Clay (The Chaucer Press) Ltd
Bungay, Suffolk

British Library Cataloguing in Publication Data

Bold, Alan
Muriel Spark.——(Contemporary writers)
1. Spark, Muriel——Criticism and
interpretation
I. Title   II. Series
823'.914   PR6037.P29Z/

ISBN 0-416-40360-3

Library of Congress Cataloging in Publication Data

Bold, Alan Norman, 1943–
Muriel Spark.
(Contemporary writers)
Bibliography: p.
1. Spark, Muriel—Criticism and interpretation.
I. Title.   II. Series.
PR6037.P29Z57   1986   823'.914   86-12671
ISBN 0-416-40360-3 (pbk.)

CONTENTS

GENERAL EDITORS' PREFACE

The contemporary is a country which we all inhabit, but there is little agreement as to its boundaries or its shape. The serious writer is one of its most sensitive interpreters, but criticism is notoriously cautious in offering a response or making a judgement. Accordingly, this continuing series is an endeavour to look at some of the most important writers of our time, and the questions raised by their work. It is, in effect, an attempt to map the contemporary, to describe its aesthetic and moral topography.

The series came into existence out of two convictions. One was that, despite all the modern pressures on the writer and on literary culture, we live in a major creative time, as vigorous and alive in its distinctive way as any that went before. The other was that, though criticism itself tends to grow more theoretical and apparently indifferent to contemporary creation, there are grounds for a lively aesthetic debate. This series, which includes books written from various standpoints, is meant to provide a forum for that debate. By design, some of those who have contributed are themselves writers, willing to respond to their contemporaries; others are critics who have brought to the discussion of current writing the spirit of contemporary criticism or simply a conviction, forcibly and coherently argued, for the contemporary significance of their subjects. Our aim, as the series develops, is to continue to explore the works of major post-war writers – in fiction, drama and poetry – over an international range, and thereby to illuminate not only those works but also in some degree the artistic, social and moral assumptions on which they rest. Our wish is that, in their very variety of approach and emphasis, these books will stimulate interest in and understanding of the vitality of a living literature which, because it is contemporary, is especially ours.

Norwich, England

MALCOLM BRADBURY
CHRISTOPHER BIGSBY

PREFACE AND
ACKNOWLEDGEMENTS

Listening to the heroine of *The Prime of Miss Jean Brodie* inventively enlarging a story, Sandy Stranger is 'fascinated by this method of making patterns with facts'. So is Muriel Spark, whose novels often explore the concept of fictional truth. After introducing the author in the first chapter, this study comments on all her novels to date – from *The Comforters* (1957) to *The Only Problem* (1984) – in an attempt to see how Mrs Spark brings a poetic vision to her perception of what passes for reality. Fleur Talbot, the autobiographical heroine of *Loitering with Intent*, observes, 'It is not to be supposed that the stamp and feeling of a novel can be conveyed by an intellectual summary.' Noting this I have tried to indicate Mrs Spark's overall imaginative approach while recognizing the special merits of particular titles.

I would like to thank Craig Tenney, of Harold Ober Associates, for advice on the Bibliography; and Malcolm Bradbury for some valuable comments on the typescript.

Extracts from the works of Muriel Spark are reprinted by permission of Harold Ober Associates Inc., copyright © 1986 by Copyright Administration Ltd.

A NOTE ON THE TEXTS

Page references to quotations from the fiction of Muriel Spark are to the British paperback editions unless otherwise stated. The following abbreviations have been used for the novels (which are listed in chronological order).

C	*The Comforters* (London: Macmillan, 1957)
R	*Robinson*
MM	*Memento Mori*
BPR	*The Ballad of Peckham Rye*
B	*The Bachelors*
PMJB	*The Prime of Miss Jean Brodie*
GSM	*The Girls of Slender Means*
MG	*The Mandelbaum Gate*
PI	*The Public Image*
DS	*The Driver's Seat*
ND	*Not to Disturb*
HER	*The Hothouse by the East River*
AC	*The Abbess of Crewe*
T	*The Takeover*
TR	*Territorial Rights*
LI	*Loitering with Intent*
OP	*The Only Problem* (London: The Bodley Head, 1984)

1

'POET AND DREAMER'

It has been Muriel Spark's singular achievement as a novelist to synthesize the linguistic cunning of poetry with the seeming credibility of prose. One of the most self-conscious of stylists, Spark has a fondness for scattering poetic quotations, like clues, throughout her fiction and it is no accident that several of the poets quoted are Metaphysical in technique or metaphysical in tone. Dr Johnson's controversial essay on Cowley (*Lives of the Poets*, 1779–81) suggested that in Metaphysical verse 'heterogeneous ideas are yoked by violence together', a remark that acquires a novel application in Spark's treatment of murder, terrorism, blackmail, fraud and other crimes against the individual. Her subjects, frequently dislocated by large doses of black comedy, are her contemporaries, who coexist with the author (or her representatives) in a world whose sublime ideals tend in practice to become ridiculous.

By way of recognizing antecedents, Spark's second novel *Robinson* (1958) alludes in conversation to one of Donne's *Devotions* (*R*, p. 22), while her longest novel, *The Mandelbaum Gate* (1965), quotes Donne's song 'Goe and Catch a Falling Starre' (*MG*, p. 47). Gerard Manley Hopkins, whose 'The Wreck of the Deutschland' undermines the Kensington scenario of *The Girls of Slender Means* (1963), is a more modern poet who showed Spark one way of applying a metaphysical manner to a narrative matter. Spark was a published poet when commissioned, at the age of 36, to write a novel, and her reservations about

11

realism encouraged her to employ a poetic strategy when composing fiction. As a poetically inclined novelist she renewed the Metaphysical mode by using the resources of modernism; her metaphorical density, range of conceit and intellectual agility draw profitably on the work of T. S. Eliot, who was, coincidentally, responsible for restoring the reputation of Donne and his disciples in an essay ('The Metaphysical Poets', 1921) that dwells on 'a dissociation of sensibility'. In a prose both Metaphysical and modernist, Spark puts character and plot under imaginative pressure. Illusion and reality become involved in a series of comic exchanges.

One of Spark's most effective conceits is the notion that characters, in actuality as well as art, can only face facts through fiction – a situation from which she extracts wisdom as well as wit. Caroline Rose, in *The Comforters* (1957), is a novelist who rearranges her environment; January Marlow, in *Robinson*, is an author open to the idea that dreams might determine her destiny; Dougal Douglas, at the end of *The Ballad of Peckham Rye* (1960), is identified as the creator of 'a lot of cockeyed books' (*BPR*, p. 142); Fleur Talbot, the heroine of *Loitering with Intent* (1981), is a novelist who deliberately confuses fact with fiction. Most revealingly, Sandy Stranger, the girl who betrays the heroine of *The Prime of Miss Jean Brodie* (1961), lives a fantasy life by writing romantic fiction and conducting conversations with literary heroes such as Alan Breck and Mr Rochester. Sandy lives solipsistically in a world of her own making; when she retreats from the everyday world she becomes not only a nun in a convent but a literary celebrity as a result of her treatise on 'The Transfiguration of the Commonplace'. Sandy is one of Spark's fictional extensions of herself: Spark too turned her back on the Calvinistic climate of Edinburgh, renounced her former companions for a lifetime of devotion, and became a literary celebrity associated with the transfiguration of the commonplace. The similarity between the dedicated novelist and the nun is a fancy that also lurks in *The Mandelbaum Gate*.

While Spark is intensely serious about her artistic calling, she uses her craft to portray life as a divine comedy that often collapses into farce when events overwhelm expectations. In her books, appearance is deceptive by nature. Barbara Vaughan describes herself, in *The Mandelbaum Gate*, as 'the safe type' (*MG*, p. 75), Lise, in *The Driver's Seat* (1970), looks obsessively for 'my type' (*DS*, p. 35), Fleur Talbot, in *Loitering with Intent*, ponders in general on 'typology' (*LI*, p. 19) and in particular on 'a type of woman whom I had come to identify in my mind as the English Rose . . . the type sickened me' (p. 20). In the fictions containing these examples, types become increasingly hard to place in terms of the plot and the plotters within it. Spark shows that a schematic understanding of typology has no place in a comic vision that focuses on the peculiarity of each person. By joyfully exposing the eccentricities of her characters Spark contradicts the conventional classification of types: her geriatric patients (*Memento Mori*, 1959) are divided by their shared status; her bachelors (*The Bachelors*, 1960) react against their common condition; her schoolgirls (*The Prime of Miss Jean Brodie*) go their separate ways. What passes for normal in actuality becomes bizarre in the fiction of Muriel Spark.

Dealing with a period ranging from the 1930s to the present, Spark is one of the most lucid and alert of contemporary writers. Even when her characters slip into solipsism her books do not ignore world events such as the rise of Fascism (*The Prime of Miss Jean Brodie*), the Second World War and its aftermath (*The Girls of Slender Means*), the Eichmann trial and the Middle East conflict (*The Mandelbaum Gate*), the Watergate scandal (*The Abbess of Crewe*, 1974), the crisis of capitalism (*The Takeover*, 1976) and political terrorism (*Territorial Rights*, 1979). But Spark is never merely topical, for her novels are haunted by the spectre of a theological eternity. In a passage echoing Proust, Fleur Talbot addresses the reader of *Loitering with Intent*: 'When people say that nothing happens in their lives I believe them. But you must understand that everything happens to an artist; time is always redeemed, nothing is lost and wonders never cease' (*LI*, p. 83). Spark has made creative time of her own life.

*

Facts, in the fiction of Muriel Spark, are invariably open to fantastic interpretation. As a writer with an inventive approach to reality she has always been reluctant to discuss publicly in great detail the facts of her own life. Just as January Marlow, the autobiographical heroine of *Robinson*, resents a 'horrible curiosity about my private life' (*R*, p. 81) so Spark prefers to let her fiction speak for itself. Though a Catholic convert she is not an overtly confessional writer; when she uses the raw material of her own experience she smooths it into artistic shape. Another of Spark's autobiographical heroines, Fleur Talbot, represents her creator in *Loitering with Intent*: 'People often ask me where I get ideas for my novels; I can only say that my life is like that, it turns into some other experience of fiction, recognizable only to myself. . . . Such as I am, I'm an artist, not a reporter' (*LI*, p. 109).

This considerable artist was born Muriel Sarah Camberg in Edinburgh in 1918. Her Jewish father, Bernard Camberg, worked as an engineer; her mother, Sarah Elizabeth Maud (née Uezelli) was a Hertfordshire woman 'with eyes of an almost gipsy blackness'.[1] As a child Muriel Camberg spent summer holidays in Watford, where her grandmother kept a general shop (which features in the story 'The Gentile Jewesses'). Back in Edinburgh Muriel Camberg was educated at James Gillespie's Girls' School, fictionalized as Marcia Blaine School in *The Prime of Miss Jean Brodie*. An imaginative girl, Muriel wrote poetry from the age of 9 and spent her free hours in Morningside Public Library. As she subsequently explained:

> James Gillespie's Girls' School, set in solid state among the green meadows, showed an energetic faith in my literary life. I was the school's Poet and Dreamer, with appropriate perquisites and concessions. I took this for granted, and have never since quite accustomed myself to the world's indifference to art and the process of art, and to the special needs of the artist.[2]

In fact, and in fiction, Muriel Spark has remained a Poet and Dreamer. Her mature work is poetic in tone, her vision more redolent of dream (or nightmare) than of prosaic reality.

At the age of 19 Muriel Camberg left Edinburgh to go to Rhodesia, where she married S. O. Spark and gave birth to a son, Robin. Her marriage was not a success[3] though the years in Africa did enlarge Spark's understanding of the exotic, and resulted in several short stories published years after the events that prompted them: 'The Pawnbroker's Wife', 'The Go-Away Bird', 'The Seraph and the Zambesi', 'The Portobello Road', 'Bang-Bang You're Dead', 'The Curtain Blown by the Breeze'. An image of Africa is also preserved in the poem 'Like Africa', included in *Going Up To Sotheby's* (1982). The third quatrain runs:

> In him the muffled drums of forests
> Inform like dreams, and manifold
> Lynx, eagle, thorn, effect about him
> Their very night and emerald.

In 1944, having divorced her husband, Spark went to England, obtaining work at Woburn Abbey in a department of the Intelligence Service run by Sefton Delmer, a specialist in anti-Nazi propaganda. Spark recalls the deceptive nature of her duties in her supernatural New York novel *The Hothouse by the East River* (1973):

> What they are engaged with in this particular Compound is known as black propaganda and psychological warfare. This is the propagation of the Allied point of view under the guise of the German point of view; it involves a tangled mixture of damaging lies, flattering and plausible truths. (*HER*, p. 52)

Spark's war work, then, involved the presentation of fiction as fact. In her creative work she does not simply reverse this process and project fact as fiction; she teases the reader with texts that query the concept of fictional truth while recognizing that a printed work of fiction is a literary fact that need not be taken literally. Enamoured of the oxymoron, she is one of the most subtle stylists of her time, a master (or mistress) of the paradox, a literary illusionist of enormous agility.

After the war, as an artistic character in search of a suitable situation, Spark joined the staff of the *Argentor*, a trade magazine dealing with jewels and precious stones, then worked as press officer for the Soldiers', Sailors' and Airmen's Families' Association. More to her liking she was, in April 1947, appointed secretary of the Poetry Society, at that time located in Portman Square, London. With little money to sustain her, Spark lived in the Helena Club, a hostel in Lancaster Gate, to the north of Kensington Gardens. *The Girls of Slender Means* fictionalized the hostel as the May of Teck Club:

> All the nice people were poor, and few were nicer, as nice people come, than these girls at Kensington who glanced out of the windows in the early mornings to see what the day looked like, or gazed out on the green summer evenings, as if reflecting on the months ahead, on love and the relations of love. Their eyes gave out an eager-spirited light that resembled near-genius, but was youth merely. (*GSM*, p. 9)

In 1947 the new secretary of the Poetry Society was 27, 'blonde and glamorous',[4] her natural red hair turned gold by Africa.

Spark, the Poet and Dreamer from Edinburgh via Africa, became editor of the *Poetry Review* (organ of the Poetry Society) in 1948 and used her position to encourage young poets, writers of her own generation. Moreover, Spark paid, and as generously as possible, for all the poems she printed. Her promotion of a policy favourable to modernism made her a magnetic figure for her contemporaries:

> So the Editorial Office in Portman Square became a sort of literary court, never before so favourable to young poets. . . . Surrounded by the young poets like Bess by her courtiers, she would sit perched on the side of the table, her short but sturdy legs dangling down like those of a child who cannot reach the floor. . . . I think all the young poets loved her; she was so buoyant, so small. They were certainly grateful to her for opening portals hitherto closed, and they sensed her own real respect for their calling and for the craft of verse.[5]

Predictably, Spark's editorial approach was anathema to the conservative members of the Poetry Society. She was dismissed from the Poetry Society, and the *Poetry Review* of December 1948 – January 1949 came complete with a leaflet announcing the end of Spark's editorship.

Leaving the Poetry Society under a cloud, Spark stayed for a short period in St John's Wood at the home of Mr and Mrs

Christmas Humphreys. It was an odd ambiance, he being not only a barrister but an English Buddhist who supported a number of lost causes (believing, for instance, that Shakespeare's plays were written by the Earl of Oxford). To continue the work she had started with the *Poetry Review*, Spark founded *Forum*; the first issue appeared in Summer 1949, the second and last issue was co-edited with Derek Stanford, the friend with whom she collaborated on a number of publications beginning with the symposium *Tribute to Wordsworth* (1950). Stanford, with his anarchist outlook and critical acumen, was a companion she then valued. However, in the London of the late 1940s she found herself reluctantly drawn into a literary circle that contained more than its fair share of eccentrics, including Rudolph Friedmann of Zwemmer's Bookshop, caricatured as the preposterous Baron Stock in *The Comforters*, and the combative poet Herbert Palmer, the original of Percy Mannering in *Memento Mori*.

Spark's distaste for the self-indulgent literary amateurism of the period is reflected in several books that allude to the cultural life that existed in Fiztrovia, an area so called after the Fitzroy Tavern on the corner of Charlotte Street and Windmill Street. In *The Comforters* Caroline Rose and Laurence Manders go to a Soho pub where 'It was understood that every close association between two people was a perversion' (C, p. 84). In *The Girls of Slender Means* Spark places the poetaster Nicholas Farringdon in 'the pubs, The Wheatsheaf and The Gargoyle' (*GSM*, p. 57). In *Loitering with Intent* the narrator Fleur Talbot observes: 'Life on the intellectual fringe in 1949 was a universe by itself. It was something like life in Eastern Europe to-day' (*LI*, p. 47). Spark's study of Mary Shelley, *Child of Light* (1951), dedicated to Derek Stanford and completed in 1950, explicitly rejects the cultural drinkers of Fitzrovia:

> We all know (no loss to those who do not) the dilapidated Bright Young Things, phantoms from the 'twenties, who haunt the pubs of Soho as if seeking in those localities of earlier promise, some indistinct token of fulfilment like a glove inadvertently left behind them.[6]

Evidently Spark dreaded being thought of as a Bright Young Thing. She wanted to be a serious artist. The Poet and Dreamer had high aesthetic standards.

From 1949 to 1950 (when she worked part-time for the magazine *European Affairs*) Spark lived at Vicarage Gate, off Church Street, Kensington. It was her habit, at that period, to write poems in the old graveyard behind St Mary Abbots. The mood of meditation is recreated at the beginning of *Loitering with Intent* as Fleur Talbot recalls how 'One day in the middle of the twentieth century' (*LI*, p. 7) she was approached by a shy young policeman who suggested she might be guilty of loitering with intent. 'But that day in the middle of the twentieth century', Fleur admits, 'I felt more than ever how good it was to be a woman and an artist there and then' (p. 144). Spark herself was, in 1949, loitering with the intention of writing poems such as 'Elegy in a Kensington Churchyard', set in the graveyard of St Mary Abbots. The poem is addressed to a long-dead lady and ends in a series of ecstatic assertions:

> Death's a contagion: spring's a bright
> Green fit; the blight will overcome
> The plague that overcame the blight
> That laid this lady low and dumb,
>
> And laid a parish on its back
> So soon amazed, so long enticed
> Into an earthy almanack,
> And musters now the spring attack;
> Which render passive, latent Christ.

Reprinted (as are the other poems cited) in *Going Up To Sotheby's*, the poem invokes the latent Christ not simply to make a rhyme with 'enticed'. The images of death and resurrection are central to the thematic thrust of the poem which lifts the dead lady from the grave and sets her into the imaginative world of a modern woman.

Spark's taste in poetry was catholic, ranging from the traditional ballads through Metaphysical verse, Wordsworth, Emily Brontë and John Masefield, to T. S. Eliot and Dylan Thomas. In her study of *John Masefield* (1953) she said 'The Border Ballads

18

are concerned with the lyrical winding in and out of a situation; for all their repetitiveness and length, they are models of narrative economy.'[7] Spark not only used ballad techniques in her verse, she subsequently extended their narrative methods to her prose in works like *The Ballad of Peckham Rye*, as discussed on pp. 53–8. T. S. Eliot's *The Waste Land* (1922), the most influential application of modernism to poetry, provided her with a structural model in which cultural references could be counterpointed against conversational asides and pertinent observations. Dylan Thomas's 'Fern Hill', published in *Deaths and Entrances* (1946), was another favourite. Thomas's poem begins with an Edenic evocation of childhood: 'Now as I was young and easy under the apple boughs / About the lilting house and happy as the grass was green'. Spark's story 'The Portobello Road', included in *The Go-Away Bird and Other Stories* (1958), emulates Thomas's Edenic euphoria in richly lyrical prose: 'One day in my young youth at high summer, lolling with my lovely companions upon a haystack I found a needle' (*The Go-Away Bird*, p. 164).

During the summer of 1950, when she had moved to the Old Brompton Road, Spark read Baudelaire's story 'La Fanfarlo' which begins (in translation): 'Samuel Cramer, who at one time – in the hey-day of Romanticism – among other romantic follies had signed himself by the name of Manuela de Monteverde, is the contradictory off-spring of a pale German father and a brown Chilean mother.'[8] Fascinated by the characters of Cramer and La Fanfarlo, Spark featured them in two poems – 'The Ballad of the Fanfarlo' and 'The Nativity' – and in a short story that was to prove crucial to her career. 'The Ballad of the Fanfarlo', her longest poem and the title poem of her first collection *The Fanfarlo and Other Verse* (1952), begins by bringing Cramer to life in London, 'The tremerous metropolis' (*Going Up To Sotheby's*, p. 20). Though there are traffic lights and lifts there is scant sympathy with everyday reality; as Cramer is a figure taken from literature the poem has an obsessively aesthetic quality. Composed largely in the ballad metre, the work progresses indirectly through a series of dialogues with Cramer. He speaks to the traffic lights, to a steel chair, to an ether-bowl, to a little keen knife (an instrument deployed as a murder weapon in several traditional ballads), to a miller,

19

a soldier, a scholar, an observer, a businessman, the Fanfarlo and (finally) to Death. He survives the convalescent ward of No-Man's sanatorium and an encounter with his alter ego, Manuela de Monteverde, 'the fattest ghost in Christendom' (*Going Up to Sotheby's*, p. 31), before coming to a paradoxical conclusion:

> 'When the lizard mates with Pegasus
> And the lynx lies with the roe,
> Then I'll forget the black and the bright
> The high delight and the low,
> Manuela de Monteverde
> And the dancing Fanfarlo.' (p. 40)

'The Ballad of the Fanfarlo', operating at two removes from reality, reads more convincingly as a literary exercise than as a substantial achievement. Spark is obviously attempting to renew the ballad format through modernist methods:

> The new moon like a pair of surgical forceps
> With the old moon in her jaws. (p. 30)

These two lines superimpose an Eliotic image (compare Spark's obstetric simile with the 'patient etherized' at the beginning of 'The Love Song of J. Alfred Prufrock' or the surgical metaphor in Part IV of 'East Coker') on an allusion to 'Sir Patrick Spens' ('Late late yestreen I saw the new moon / Wi' the auld moon in her arm'). Spark's urban atmosphere, too, derives from early Eliot:

> The noise of a fog-horn out behind the window,
> As well as the smell of gas,
> And visible air of a metropolitan yellow. . . . (p. 26)

When Spark recast the characters of Cramer and the Fanfarlo in a prose composition, 'The Seraph and the Zambesi', the result was strikingly superior. Significantly the prose of the short story was more genuinely poetic than the verse of the poem.

'The Seraph and the Zambesi', collected in *The Go-Away Bird and Other Stories*, opens abruptly with a factual projection of a literary fantasy: 'You may have heard of Samuel Cramer, half poet, half journalist, who had to do with a dancer called the Fanfarlo' (*The Go-Away Bird*, p. 155). The first paragraph contains the supernatural suggestion that Cramer is still going strong a century after his creation in a Baudelaire tale; the second paragraph introduces a religious element as the narrator 'was sent to him because it was Christmas week and there was no room in the hotel' (p. 155). Spark thus alerts the reader to a visionary dimension in which her story unfolds not as a naturalistic narrative but as a poetic introduction to a world in which anything might happen. At the same time the supernatural is plausibly rendered: when the narrator meets him in 1946, Cramer is keeping a petrol pump a few miles south of the Zambesi River.

At Cramer's sundowner party, the narrator is introduced to Mannie, a short, dark man, and to his wife Fanny, aged around 50, with grey hair tinted blue and a face 'puckered with malaria' (p. 156). Fanny, it transpires, is Mme La Fanfarlo and Mannie is Manuela de Monteverde, Cramer's alter ego. Cramer has largely abandoned his literary career but has written a Nativity Masque for performance on Christmas Eve in his garage. At the Masque, Fanny (La Fanfarlo) is to act the part of the Virgin; Mannie (on account of his broken English) is to perform the non-speaking role of a shepherd; Cramer himself is to be the First Seraph. Miraculously, a heavenly seraph, complete with three sets of wings, turns up for the performance asserting its divine right to be itself instead of being represented by Cramer. A furious Cramer encourages troopers to throw petrol at the Seraph, whose heat causes combustion. Ironically Cramer contents himself by recalling that he is insured: 'my policy covers everything except Acts of God' (p. 162). The Seraph survives the blaze and is glimpsed at the end of the story on the Zambesi 'among the rocks that look like crocodiles and the crocodiles that look like rocks' (p. 163).

Spark set a stylistic precedent with 'The Seraph and the Zambesi', the first of her works to convey her singular tone. By using the imaginative freedom of poetry she overturns fictional conventions. Both protagonists, Cramer and the Seraph (one from literature, the other from legend) are beyond the immediate experience of the reader, yet Spark gives them a textual reality by fixing them in her fiction, by allowing them to materialize in print. In her story symbolism blends with supernaturalism, irony alternates with assertion, the vivid impression of an event dissolves into a final simile that touches on the problem of perception. Spark's poem 'Elementary' acknowledges the author's 'odd capacity for vision', a vision that treats the world as simultaneously subjective and objective. It is a vision she triumphantly applied to prose in 'The Seraph and the Zambesi' and her story shows that a prose-poem need not be synonymous with a series of purple passages. Poetry here is the formal manipulation of creative impulses as Spark brings to prose the technical repertoire of a poet. In 1951 Spark submitted 'The Seraph and the Zambesi' to the *Observer* Christmas story competition. It was awarded first place out of 6700 entries and appeared in the *Observer* of 23 December 1951; David Astor, the paper's editor, thought so highly of the piece that he came to Spark's flat at around 2 a.m. on the Sunday morning with the first copy of an issue so important to the author.

If she had achieved success by introducing an angel into her prizewinning story, Spark was still casting about for a faith to give her a spiritual sense of security. Her first volume of verse, *The Fanfarlo and Other Verse*, appeared in 1952 and the following year she was baptized as an Anglican by the Rev. C. O. Rhodes, editor of the *Church of England Newspaper*, to which Spark contributed a study of Proust, 'The Religion of an Agnostic', on 27 November 1953 – Fleur Talbot, in *Loitering with Intent*, mentions 'those long, devoted, underpaid but often well-appreciated articles I wrote for church newspapers' (*LI*, p. 109). After being confirmed by the Anglo-Catholic Bishop of Kensington, Spark began to frequent the Gloucester Road church attended by T. S. Eliot, a poet whose work she worshipped. Under the influence of John Henry Newman's *Apologia pro Vita Sua* (1864), a spiritual autobiography cited in *Loitering with Intent*, Spark then came to the conclusion that Roman Catholicism was the True Faith. In 1953 she was instructed by Father Aegius at Ealing Priory.

During this period Spark, now living at Queen's Gate, began to show signs of nervous exhaustion. In his version of this difficult time Derek Stanford claims he encouraged others to assist Spark.[9] Frank Sheed commissioned her to write a study of the Book of Job, an interest incorporated into *The Comforters* and *The Only Problem* (1984). Graham Greene, A. J. Cronin and David Astor also helped financially while Father O'Malley gave her the benefit, after her conversion, of his Jungian therapy. In 1954, the year she was received into the Roman Catholic Church by Father Philip Caraman, Alan Maclean of Macmillan commissioned her to write a novel. She went to live in a cottage near Aylesford Priory, Kent, and began work on *The Comforters*. That first novel, discussed on pp. 34–41, made creative sense of her nervous collapse and conversion.

Derek Stanford has insinuated that Spark was by no means a quietly retiring, passive Catholic convert at Aylesford Priory and that the internal evidence of her fiction does not equate her True Faith with a comfortable condition.[10] She admitted, in an interview, 'I wasn't able to work and to do any of my writing until I became a Catholic',[11] so, like Newman, she appreciated, above all, the disciplined authority of the Roman Catholic Church. Yet, with the exception of Jean Taylor in *Memento Mori*, none of her Roman Catholic characters is truly sympathetic. Georgina Hogg, in *The Comforters*, is a repulsively dogmatic Catholic; the eponymous hero of *Robinson* is an arrogant escapist at odds with the Church that trained him; Ronald Bridges, the epileptic graphologist of *The Bachelors*, says, 'As a Catholic I loathe all other Catholics' (*B*, p. 79); Sandy Stranger, who betrays the heroine of *The Prime of Miss Jean Brodie*, finds in the Catholic Church 'quite a number of Fascists much less agreeable than Miss Brodie' (*PMJB*, p. 125); *The Abbess of Çrewe* places political corruption in a convent; Cuthbert Plaice, a Jesuit priest in *The Takeover*, is seen 'shifting about with excitement in his chair as if he were sexually as much as pastorally roused' (*T*, p. 12). Is nothing sacred? Not, seemingly, for Spark's satirical temperament. According to a report on her life in Rome,

> Even now she cannot wholly accept the doctrines of her church. She attends Mass regularly in Rome, but always arrives after the sermons have been delivered because 'I can't stand third-rate productions'. Moreover, she believes 'if Christ suffered for the whole world, then we should be finished suffering'.[12]

As a novelist Spark uses Roman Catholicism as an ideal against which lesser concepts can be judged. If individuals are generally unworthy of Spark's True Faith then she shows they have little trouble adjusting to a series of false faiths: Baron Stock's occultism in *The Comforters*, Tom Wells's futurology in *Robinson*, Dougal Douglas's diabolism in *The Ballad of Peckham Rye*, Patrick Seton's spiritualism in *The Bachelors*, Jean Brodie's fascism in *The Prime of Miss Jean Brodie*, Nicholas Farringdon's bohemianism in *The Girls of Slender Means*, Adolf Eichmann's anti-Semitism in *The Mandelbaum Gate*, Annabel Christopher's cinematic eroticism in *The Public Image* (1968), Lise's voluntarism in *The Driver's Seat*, Hubert Mallindaine's paganism in *The Takeover*, Sir Quentin Oliver's chemically induced fanaticism in *Loitering with Intent* and Harvey Gotham's academic isolationism in *The Only Problem*. 'I have never', says Fleur Talbot in *Loitering with Intent*, 'known an artist who at some time in his life has not come into conflict with pure evil' (*LI*, p. 120). The evil that men, and women, do is scrutinized by Spark in her novels, most of which mention blackmail, many of which feature betrayal, some of which include murder. Though her verbal touch is light, Spark implies a moral ethos in her novels.

Muriel Spark was 39 when her first novel was published. It was praised by Evelyn Waugh,[13] who explored a similar theme in *The Ordeal of Gilbert Pinfold* (1957). Settling in Camberwell, after completing *The Comforters*, Spark swiftly fulfilled her fictional promise by publishing *Robinson*, *Memento Mori*, *The Ballad of Peckham Rye*, *The Bachelors* and *The Prime of Miss Jean Brodie* – the last of these was first published in the *New Yorker* of 14 October 1961. On 2 October 1962 the New Arts Theatre Club of London presented, as its inaugural play, Spark's *Doctors of Philosophy*. As in Pirandello's classic *Sei personaggi in cerca d'autore* (produced in London in 1922 as *Six Characters in Search of an Author*), *Doctors of Philosophy* makes great dramatic play of the nature of role-playing, the fusion (and confusion) of appearance and reality. Some of Spark's characters know they are acting parts in a theatrical drama and so are self-conscious about the act of perception. Mrs S., the articulate servant whose erudition is more than equal to the collective wisdom of the assembled academics, tells Leonara that there is no broom cupboard in reality, only 'a pure idea somewhere behind the scenes'.[14] Leonara, who has a PhD in Classics, has 'A definite sense of being observed and listened to by an audience'.[15] She disturbs Annie Wood by shaking the stage set to reveal that external reality is, in a creative context, an illusion. Spark manipulates the characters in a comedy of confusion complicated by the use of identical first names – there are three Charlies in the play (two PhDs, one lorry-driver). Some of the verbal exchanges are extremely witty, as witness the following:

> CATHERINE. Daphne's young friend, Charlie Weston. My cousin, Mrs Wood. Charlie is a nuclear-physicist, Annie, he's doing secret work.
> ANNIE. Really? Tell me all about it.[16]

Although her play was applauded, by critics as well as by theatre-goers, Spark did not persist with dramatic work, preferring to concentrate on the novel as the form most suitable to her gifts.

In 1962 Spark left London, partly because she felt that her literary fame and fortune had separated her from her former friends: 'It was painful to be with them, simply because I felt like a sort of reproach to them – and they to me.'[17] For three years she lived in the USA, making use of an office put at her disposal by the *New Yorker*. In 1966 she settled in Rome, where she still lives.

Spark's popular reputation is immense: her novels are constantly in print and occasionally are interpreted through other media. *The Prime of Miss Jean Brodie* has been a stage-play (dramatized by Jay Presson, featuring Vanessa Redgrave in the London production), a feature film (of 1969, starring Maggie Smith), and a television series (with Geraldine McEwan as Jean Brodie); *The Driver's Seat* (in 1975) and *The Abbess of Crewe* (in 1977, retitled *Nasty Habits*) have both been recreated as feature films, the former starring Elizabeth Taylor as Lise, the latter Glenda Jackson as Alexandra. Some critics, however, have carped at her achievements, one insisting on the epithet 'minor',[18] another describing her (on the basis of her early novels) as 'a talented literary confectioner, a combination of Firbank and Compton-Burnett'.[19] Spark's economy of artistic means has undoubtedly prejudiced critics who automatically equate length with depth. Yet Spark remains an enormously important writer, blessed with a poetic vision of modern life as a divine comedy of errors. Instead of parading her wisdom, she concentrates on wit: the result, in *The Prime of Miss Jean Brodie*, is a masterpiece of modern literature.

The genesis of Spark's style is partly geographical, as she has acknowledged. Growing up in Edinburgh she was constantly surprised by the city's way of accommodating nature and art: 'To have a great primitive black crag [the Castle Rock] rising up in the middle of populated streets of commerce, stately squares and winding closes, is like the statement of an unmitigated fact preceded by "nevertheless".'[20] Spark's writing frequently admits the nevertheless principle; astonishing events regularly occur as a matter of narrative fact (an angel in Africa, a devil in Peckham). Spark has also said:

> I am certainly a writer of Scottish formation and of course think of myself as such. I think to describe myself as a 'Scottish Writer' might be ambiguous as one wouldn't know if 'Scottish' applied to the writer or the writing. Then there is the complicated question of whether people of mixed inheritance, like myself, can call themselves Scottish. Some Scots deny it. But Edinburgh where I was born and my father was born has definitely had an effect on my mind, my prose style and my ways of thought.[21]

Indeed, a macabre element in Spark's work derives from Scotland, where the supernatural persists from the ballads, through Burns, Scott, Hogg and Stevenson, to Spark herself. The influence of James Hogg's *The Private Memoirs and Confessions of a Justified Sinner* (1824) can be discerned in *The Ballad of Peckham Rye* (see pp. 53–8) and Stevenson's *The Strange Case of Dr Jekyll and Mr Hyde* (1886) must have made a profound impression on a writer fascinated by the coexistence of good and evil. Above all, though, the ballads helped to shape Spark's prose with its timeshifts, its combination of the natural and supernatural, its atmosphere of enchantment.

One of Spark's finest stories, 'The Portobello Road' in *The Go-Away Bird and Other Stories*, draws on the ballad tradition – and does so self-consciously, since it carries an allusion to the 'Borderland' (*The Go-Away Bird*, p. 164), where so many Scottish ballads are set. The narrator, known as Needle because she once found a needle in a haystack, perceives herself as a revenant rather than a disembodied ghost: though the victim of a murder and definitely dead she 'did not altogether depart this world' (p. 167). In the traditional ballads revenants linger in the world for love, for revenge, for peace of mind. In Spark's story the revenant remains out of curiosity. That humorous interpretation of a great tradition is what makes Spark special; she renews the past by means of a modernist sensibility that glories in irony, paronomasia, parody, psychological shock. When the scene shifts from physical youth to supernatural maturity, Spark metaphorically extends the narrator's nickname, for Needle is suddenly 'threading among the crowds' (p. 165) in Portobello Road. A flashback to Africa establishes that George, one of Needle's trinity of childhood friends, has married a 'dark brown' woman (p. 171). Back in England, Needle goes to Kent to meet George, who now announces his intention of marrying Kathleen. Easily shocked, 'because of my Scottish upbringing' (p. 175), Needle tells George she will reveal all. George 'looked as if he would murder me and he did' (p. 185). He stuffs hay into Needle's mouth and hides her body in a haystack. The Haystack Murder gives rise to a ghastly pun in a newspaper headline: '"Needle" is found: in haystack!' (p. 185). Spark has used a ballad scenario with a linguistic sophistication unknown to the oral bards of tradition.

While Spark's novels drop the names of many poets and are punctuated with verse quotations, references to other prose writers are limited. She admires Mary Shelley, who, as a girl, spent some time near Dundee, a fact noted approvingly by Spark in her *Child of Light*: 'Mary was right in looking back on her visit to Scotland as a period of creative gestation; the comparative vastness of the hills and wooded landscapes evoked a latent response to actuality.'[22] Spark identifies other specific prose influences as Proust, Newman and Max Beerbohm.[23] From Proust she learned how to take liberties with time (her novels are full of flashbacks and flashforwards) and how to draw attention to the writer's creative participation in a text. From Newman's *Apologia pro Vita Sua* she derived an intellectual clarity with regard to spiritual issues. In Beerbohm's *Zuleika Dobson* (1911) she discerned a conversational ease and a descriptive vivacity. Evelyn Waugh's impact on Spark has been exaggerated, perhaps on the assumption that *The Comforters* thematically duplicated *The Ordeal of Gilbert Pinfold*; but though the two books were published in the same year, 1957, Spark's was finished first and Waugh read it in proof while working on his schizophrenic fiction.[24]

The literary evidence certainly demonstrates that Spark has treated fictional prose as a poetic mode. In Pope's *The Rape of the Lock* (1717), for example, the elegant surface of the verse is suddenly disturbed by a reference to grim reality:

> Meanwhile, declining from the noon of day,
> The sun obliquely shoots his burning ray;
> The hungry judges soon the sentence sign,
> And wretches hang that jurymen may dine. . . . (III, 19–22)

Similar shock tactics are employed by Spark in her novels (and in stories such as 'The Black Madonna', in which liberal pretensions are confounded by racial prejudice). Describing the Victory in Europe celebrations in London in *The Girls of Slender Means*, Spark contrasts the elegance of the royal family with the collective sexual congress of the crowd:

> The royal family waved, turned to go, lingered and waved again, and finally disappeared. Many strange arms were twined round strange bodies. Many liaisons, some permanent, were formed in the night, and numerous infants of experimental variety, delightful in hue of skin and racial structure, were born to the world in the due cycle of nine months after. (*GSM*, p. 17)

The Prime of Miss Jean Brodie takes the privileged girls of Marcia Blaine School on a winter walk through the civilized city of Edinburgh and confronts them with a sorry spectacle:

> They had come to the end of Lauriston Place, past the fire station, where they were to get on a tram-car to go to tea with Miss Brodie in her flat at Churchhill. A very long queue of men lined this part of the street. They were without collars, in shabby suits. They were talking and spitting and smoking little bits of cigarette held between middle finger and thumb.
>
> 'We shall cross here,' said Miss Brodie and herded the set across the road.
>
> Monica Douglas whispered, 'They are the Idle.' (*PMJB*, p. 39)

The incident has touches reminiscent of Eliot, who watched 'lonely men in shirt sleeves' (in 'The Love Song of J. Alfred Prufrock'), noted 'a city block. ... And short square fingers stuffing pipes' ('Preludes'), and observed 'Twisted faces from the bottom of the street' ('Morning at the Window'). The passage represents a real scene transfigured by an outlook shaped through modernist poetry.

At the end of *The Abbess of Crewe*, Alexandra gives instructions for the preparation of selective transcripts of her tape-recordings. Instead of the Nixonian euphemism 'Expletive deleted' she opts for the phrase 'Poetry deleted' (*AC*, p. 106). If the poetic tone were deleted from Spark's novels the loss would be calamitous. As it is, a poetic consciousness informs the fiction. At its most obvious this poetic approach results in a number of fine phrases: in *The Bachelors*, Patrick Seton is 'frail as a sapling birch with rain on its silver head' (*B*, p. 143); in *The Girls of Slender Means* 'Jane's life began to sprout once more, green with possibility' (*GSM*, p. 98); in *The Mandelbaum Gate*, an experience embedded in Freddy Hamilton's memory is seen

> suddenly returning on a day when the sun was a crimson disc between the bare branches of Kensington Gardens, and the skaters on the Round Pond were all splashed over the heads and arms with red light, as they beat their mittens together and skimmed the dark white ice under the sky. (*MG*, p. 250)

Again, *The Mandelbaum Gate* relates how Freddy 'experienced the sensation of one who has had a disturbing dream, and wakes with relief to discover the telephone is in fact ringing beside his bed, and answers it, only to hear disturbing news' (p. 62). Spark's ability to make her novels read like 'disturbing news' is a poetic gift which depends on subtle linguistic methods and an imaginative control over her material.

Edmund Wilson, in his essay 'Is Verse a Dying Technique?', distinguishes between verse and poetry by regarding the former as a prosodic matter and the latter as a visionary manner, and he cites Flaubert's desire (expressed in a letter of 27 March 1853 to Louise Colet) 'to give verse-rhythm to prose, yet to leave it prose and very much prose'. While the epics of Neruda, Pound, Williams,

Zukofsky, MacDiarmid and others refute his general contention that the long poem is a thing of the past, Wilson's conclusions have a particular application to Spark's work:

> the technique of prose is inevitably tending more and more to take over the material which had formerly provided the subjects for compositions in verse. . . . The technique of prose today seems thus to be absorbing the technique of verse. . . . The point is that literary techniques are tools, which the masters of the craft have to alter in adapting them to fresh uses.[25]

Modernist prose, as initiated by Flaubert and evolved by Proust and Joyce, uses language not as a crude means to a predictable narrative end but as a ritual defining a religion of art. Roman Catholic by conversion and poetic by inclination, Spark subscribes to the aesthetic religion of modernism, uses her verbal material ritualistically to create an atmosphere in which events do not occur according to a conventional sequential logic but appear to satisfy the author's imaginative needs. She produces a sacramental aura, a 'Transfiguration of the Commonplace', to use the title of Sandy Stranger's psychological treatise in *The Prime of Miss Jean Brodie*.

Spark has said that she first resisted the novel because she thought it 'a lazy way of writing poetry'.[26] Her achievement has been to make the novel a dazzlingly poetic mode through layers of language. Though never outrageously experimental in the manner of, say, the later Joyce, she uses parody with verve: the epistolary origins of the English novel are parodied in the course of *The Comforters*, romantic fiction is parodied in the adventures concocted by Sandy Stranger and Jenny Gray in *The Prime of Miss Jean Brodie*, the fairytale format is parodied in *The Girls of Slender Means*, the happy ending is parodied in many novels that end with a catalogue indicating the fate of the main characters. She is an accomplished punster, as witness Barbara Vaughan's 'state of conflict' (*MG*, p. 75) in Israel in *The Mandelbaum Gate*; she puts irony and paradox to great effect in almost all her novels. She preserves such a purity of diction that when characters in *Loitering with Intent* are quoted using the words 'fuck . . . arse . . . tits' (*LI*, pp. 56, 57, 75) the conversational coarseness points up the poise of the descriptive prose. She can condense her prose into aphoristic affirmations, as in *Loitering with Intent*:

> Without a mythology, a novel is nothing. The true novelist, one who understands the work as a continuous poem, is a myth-maker, and the wonder of the art resides in the endless different ways of telling a story, and the methods are mythological by nature. (p. 100)

In the same novel she (through Fleur Talbot) declares, with justice, 'I conceive everything poetically' (p. 21).

By imposing a verbal discipline on her emotions, Spark gives a structural stability to her prose. Her poem 'Against the Transcendentalists' dismisses the rhetoric of romanticism by dissociating the author from 'Delphic insanity,/Drunkenness and discrepancy' and observing 'There is more of everything than poetry'. In the place of romanticism Spark advocates 'the arts of satire and of ridicule. And I see no other living art form for the future.'[27] Charmian Colston, the old novelist in *Memento Mori*, says 'the art of fiction is very like the practice of deception' (*MM*, p. 187). Spark's knowledge that fiction, by its deceptive form, requires an act of faith from the reader is the source of many of her fantasies. She implies, paradoxically, that the truth lies in her texts.

Like Gerard Manley Hopkins, Spark subscribes privately to the notion that the world is charged with the grandeur of God. Still, she prefers to manipulate characters indifferent to this grandeur. Her heroines, including autobiographical ones such as Caroline Rose, Barbara Vaughan and Fleur Talbot, are self-centred creatures temperamentally inclined to solipsism. Her male characters tend to be corrupt, blackmailers or worse. Spark's vision, then, confronts evil as a force that motivates humankind and she exposes, satirically, characters who squander their God-given (according to her faith) gifts for self-gratification or material gain. Those who find Spark's stories fanciful in their surfeit of wickedness have no trouble accepting as factual a newspaper item like the following:

> A conman got more than £200,000 out of wealthy and titled Christians by pretending the money would destroy an evil satanic ring, a court heard yesterday.

Derry Mainwaring Knight used a gullible rector to collect money from people like Viscount Hampden, the Earl of March – owner of Goodwood racecourse – and Mrs Susan Sainsbury, wife of the millionaire Tory MP, Mr Timothy Sainsbury, Maidstone Crown Court was told.

Knight, a record producer, allegedly told the Rev. John Baker, of Newick, East Sussex, that he had been initiated by sacrifice into satanism by his grandmother at the age of eight and had been born to hold the highest office in his order.[28]

That scenario could have been scripted by Spark, who has observed 'how sharp and lucid fantasy can be when it is deliberately intagliated on the surface of realism.'[29] Little wonder that Fleur Talbot protests (albeit facetiously) in *Loitering with Intent*, 'When I first started writing people used to say my novels were exaggerated. They never were exaggerated, merely aspects of realism' (*LI*, p. 64). The statement can stand if the epithet 'visionary' qualifies certain aspects of realism.

The struggle between good and evil, always present in Spark's work, has its moralistic point. Ultimately, though, the moral she draws is a poetic one, a celebration of verbal virtuosity as an antidote to the poisonous spread of atrocious acts. By saturating her prose in poetic qualities she endorses Eliot's assurance that there is 'a lifetime burning in every moment' ('East Coker'). For Spark the world can be renewed through imaginative means, which is why she opposes the defeatism of determinism. In her poem 'Canaan' she issues her artistic credo in a succinct quatrain:

> No year is twice the same, nor has occurred
> Before. We bandy by the name of grief,
> Grief which is like no other. Not a leaf
> Repeats itself, we only repeat the word.

It is the poetic magic of the word that makes Spark an entertainingly original writer.

Even where her novels place unsympathetic characters in claustrophobically close situations she generally resolves the conflict through her edifying endings, her final flourishes that bring her books to a poetic conclusion. There is the 'curious rejoicing' (*The*

Comforters), the feeling that 'all things are possible' (*Robinson*), the wish 'to magnify the Lord' (*Memento Mori*), the 'cloud of green and gold' (*The Ballad of Peckham Rye*), the 'deep repose' (*The Bachelors*), the memory of 'a Miss Jean Brodie in her prime' (*The Prime of Miss Jean Brodie*), the girl 'sturdy and bare-legged on the dark grass' (*The Girls of Slender Means*), the 'medieval maze of streets' (*The Mandelbaum Gate*), the 'harking image of former and former seas' (*The Public Image*), the 'fear and pity, pity and fear' (*The Driver's Seat*), the sunlight 'laughing on the walls' (*Not to Disturb*), the 'lithe cloud of unknowing' (*The Hothouse by the East River*), the 'cornfield of sublimity' (*The Abbess of Crewe*), the 'kindly fruits of the earth' (*The Takeover*), the 'roses in the garden' (*Territorial Rights*), the 'grace of God' (*Loitering with Intent*), the 'little wilderness' (*The Only Problem*). If Spark suggests that the world is short on values she nevertheless ensures that her last words bestow a visionary blessing on it.

2

THE FIRST FIVE NOVELS

'A first novel', the publisher Revisson Doe assures Fleur Talbot in *Loitering with Intent*, 'is after all a pure experiment' (*LI*, p. 96). On her own admission, Muriel Spark wrote her first novel, *The Comforters* (1957), as an experimental exploration of the formal nature of fictional truth. In an interview with Frank Kermode she explained candidly:

> I was asked to write a novel, and I didn't think much of novels – I thought it was an inferior way of writing. So I wrote a novel to work out the technique first, to sort of make it all right with myself to write a novel at all – a novel about writing a novel, about writing a novel sort of thing, you see.[30]

Just as the narrator of Proust's *A la recherche du temps perdu* closes by resolving to write the book the reader has before him, so Spark's heroine Caroline Rose is portrayed, in the final pages of *The Comforters*, as a woman intent on writing a novel about 'Characters in a novel' (*C*, p. 231). The last sentence of Spark's book (reflecting on how a mutilated letter subsequently appears intact in a novel) makes it clear that Caroline Rose's first novel is to be *The Comforters*. This ultimate twist completes the teasing of the reader, who has been seduced into believing a story eventually exposed as a structure supporting a fictional fantasy. Nevertheless the fiction has an epistemological validity. As Spark herself says, 'I don't claim that my novels are truth – I claim that they are fiction, out of which a kind of truth emerges.[31]

Before she is identified as the author of the fiction in which she features, Caroline Rose is categorized as the central character in the third-personal narrative. She is working on a study of contemporary fiction, *Form in the Modern Novel*, and 'having difficulty with the chapter on realism' (p. 59). In the relentlessly realist novel the author is made in the all-seeing image of Bishop Berkeley's God: material objects (including individuals) only exist by virtue of divine perception. Spark evidently enjoys playing games with this notion. Georgina Hogg, the villainess of the piece, has a habit of disappearing from view when not directly involved in the action; Caroline Rose realizes that Georgina has 'no private life whatsoever' (p. 212), only a role to play in an aesthetic ritual. Caroline herself, as a Catholic, objects to the deterministic nature of realism, telling her boyfriend Laurence Manders, 'I won't be involved in this fictional plot. . . . I intend to stand aside and see if the novel has any real form apart from this artificial plot. I happen to be a Christian' (p. 117).

The Comforters does have 'real form', though the format is ingeniously ambiguous. It uncannily simulates the neurotic nature of Caroline Rose's obsessions by making her function as a plausible character anxiously resisting the pull of an absorbing plot. Evelyn Waugh recognized Spark's brilliant solution to the problem of conveying neurosis in the novel. When he first read *The Comforters* he was working on his own schizophrenic fiction *The Ordeal of Gilbert Pinfold* (1957). Thanking the pseudonymous novelist Gabriel Fielding (Alan Barnsley, to whom *The Comforters* is partly dedicated) for sending him a copy of Spark's 'remarkable book', he noted 'The mechanics of the hallucinations are well managed. These particularly interested me as I am myself engaged on a similar subject.'[32] Writing to Ann Fleming, wife of Ian Fleming, Waugh expressed some alarm about the similarities between *The Comforters* and *The Ordeal of Gilbert Pinfold*:

> I have been sent proofs of a very clever first novel by a lady named Muriel Sparks [*sic*]. The theme is a Catholic novelist suffering from hallucinations, hearing voices – rather disconcerting. It will appear quite soon. I am sure people will think it is by me. Please contradict such assertions.[33]

In fact, Spark's fiction could only have been by herself, for the book touches on a number of subjects she has triumphantly made her own as a novelist (the repulsively pious Catholic, the bond of blackmail, the Gothic chill of the occult, the false faiths that encroach on a true faith). Moreover, the raw material of *The Comforters* was provided by the reality of Spark's own experience.

The fictional Caroline Rose is certainly based on the facts of Spark's life in the early 1950s. Like Spark in 1953–4, Caroline has 'her family on the Jewish side' (*C*, p. 37), has 'been in Africa' (p. 49), has 'a literary reputation' (p. 71). In 1953 Spark was working on a book about the Book of Job[34] while Caroline is struggling with her study of form in the modern novel. While dwelling on her decision to adopt the Roman Catholic faith, Spark lived in a flat at Queen's Gate, as does Caroline (p. 67). Spark received instruction at Ealing Benedictine Priory from Father Aegius, who gave her bodily sustenance from hot milk and biscuits;[35] Caroline goes to a Benedictine priory to receive instruction from Father Jerome, who sends the lay brother to her 'with a glass of milk and biscuits' (p. 64). Spark worked on *The Comforters* in 1955 while living near Allington Castle, Kent, in a cottage owned by the Carmelite Friars of Aylesford Priory. Caroline's retreat is the Pilgrim Centre of St Philumena, Liverpool, next door to a convent.

During the period 1953–4 Muriel Spark was apparently displaying psychological withdrawal symptoms as a result of her change in faith. After she had been received into the Roman Catholic Church in 1954, Father Frank O'Malley, Rector of St Ethelreda's, gave her the benefit of Jungian therapy for six months: Evelyn Waugh heard 'she was very dotty and got over it'.[36] Caroline Rose's psychological problems are vividly described, the narrative recalling 'a time when her brain was like a Guy Fawkes night, ideas cracking off in all directions, dark idiot-figures jumping round a fiery junk-heap in the centre' (p. 34). When the publishers Macmillan commissioned Spark to write a novel in 1954 Spark was a Catholic convert who was subsequently to acknowledge: 'I wasn't able to work and to do any of my writing until I became a Catholic.'[37] In writing *The Comforters* Spark made sense of her own psychological and spiritual crises by subjecting them to an artistic discipline. An admirer of Eliot, she found an aesthetically demanding objective correlative by embodying her emotions in Caroline, who finally identifies the voices she hears as messages prompted by creative pressure rather than schizophrenic phantoms.

Establishing a precedent for her other novels, Spark contradicts physical appearance by the facts of her fiction. Louisa Jepp, modelled on Spark's maternal grandmother,[38] is introduced in the first chapter of *The Comforters* as a woman of 78 living in a cottage in Sussex. Her discussion about bread with the baker, Mr Webster, seems perfectly routine, though it is rapidly revealed – in a letter from Laurence Manders, BBC sports commentator, to his former fiancée Caroline – that Louisa is a septuagenarian smuggler, leader of a gang of criminals. Appearance, Spark implies, is illusory: the little old lady is an accomplished crook and the baker helps her by hiding diamonds in his loaves of bread. Formally, letters play an important part in *The Comforters*, recalling the epistolary origins of the English novel (appropriately so since Caroline is a student of the structure of the novel). Laurence's letter also imparts the information that he and Caroline have a mutual bookseller friend called the Baron and that Georgina Hogg, currently at St Philumena's, 'suffers from chronic righteousness, exerts a sort of moral blackmail' (C, p. 23). Inevitably, given the epistolary motif that runs through the narrative, Georgina Hogg uses letters to back her moral blackmail: she intercepts Laurence's letter to Caroline and receives an anonymous letter informing her that her husband Mervyn has (by changing his surname to Hogarth) bigamously married Eleanor (who has since divorced him and become the Baron's mistress, thus complicating the plot entertainingly).

If Roman Catholicism is, for Caroline Rose, the True Faith, then she is (like her creator Muriel Spark) too shrewd to accept other Catholics as automatically blessed by the religious faith they flaunt. According to Caroline, Georgina Hogg is 'simply a Catholic atrocity, like the tin medals and bleeding hearts' (p. 113). Catering Warden of St Philumena's, Georgina is an ignorant 'cradle Catholic' (p. 39), a woman who supposes she is the ripe apple of Our Lady's eye. Georgina is convinced she was sent to St Philumena's by Our Lady – 'I know it was Our Lady's message' (p. 33) – who thus made a miracle of the coming of the Catering

Warden, though the reader knows from Laurence's letter that it was his mother, Lady Helena Manders, who put Georgina in her culinary place. Repelled by Georgina's physical obesity and spiritual vacuity, Caroline reflects 'that Mrs Hogg could easily become an obsession, the demon of that carnal hypocrisy which struck her mind whenever she came across a gathering of Catholics or Jews engaged in their morbid communal pleasures' (p. 39). By making Caroline, a Catholic and a Jew, reject her spiritual and ethnic associates Spark is sending out signals that the reader should take nothing for granted.

Thematically, *The Comforters* explores an issue underlying Spark's entire output: the spiritual isolation of the individual. Neither religion nor race, it seems, can confer a sense of community on the heroine; she is alone in a claustrophobically crowded world. Deriving its title from the discomfortable comforters in the Book of Job, the novel puts Caroline in a distressing predicament. At St Philumena's she comes up against Georgina, 'a psychological thug' (p. 77) with an unsettling attitude. Back in her tiny London flat, from the balcony of which she can see the whole length of Queen's Gate, Caroline hears voices, a whole 'chorus of voices' (p. 43), preceded by the sound of a typewriter which then records her own thoughts. Thus she derives no comfort from being in religious retreat, can find no comfort in the solitude of her flat where she is haunted by the Typing Ghost. Like Job – the Book of Job is cited once in the text (p. 111) – Caroline has to rely on her own spiritual resources. Initially confused because she dreads being manoeuvred like a character in a novel, she decides to oppose the destiny predetermined for her. 'It's a matter of asserting free will' (p. 108), she tells Laurence Manders. Caroline Rose is the first of Spark's intensely independent intellectual heroines.

In the context of a novel about a novelist writing a novel, Caroline's assertion of free will is paradoxical, for she is simultaneously a creator and a character, an artist and an emblem. Beyond her fictional presence, too, lurks the authentic authorial figure of Muriel Spark. The conundrum forces the reader to receive the novel as both an ingeniously plotted tale and a self-consciously literary text. The reader is thus kept at a distance, edged away from empathy. Discussing the pictorial equivalent of this distancing device, E. H. Gombrich claims that 'What moves the *trompe-l'oeil* into the vicinity of art is precisely the connoisseur's vicarious participation in the artist's skill.'[39] By imposing on the reader her own creative act of perception, Spark announces her freedom of aesthetic choice. *The Comforters* makes a literary exhibition of itself through its modernist structure – its insistence on its existence as a literary end in itself – and poetic tone. The poetic approach is not confined to the charged use of language that allows Spark to refer to 'a silence so still you could hear a moth breathe' (*C*, p. 127) and to the 'long bruised sleep' (p. 129) which Caroline endures after her car accident. In addition to this textual richness there is the linguistic treatment of the text as a medium containing provocative contrasts: the hypertense heroine and her unedifying environment; the Catholic ritual and the everyday routine; the eternal contrast between appearance and actuality.

Caroline may be spiritually apart in (as well as a part of) the novel she eventually constructs, but she is also, as the creator of *The Comforters* (courtesy of Muriel Spark), in control, albeit retrospectively. The other characters are isolated by their egocentric aberrations. Caroline's unreliable friend Baron Stock (note the pun on barren stock) has his suspect bookshop in Charing Cross but is also the London agent for Louisa Jepp's smuggling racket and an addict of occultism, one of Spark's false faiths. Mervyn Hogarth, another member of the smuggling ring, is a bigamist who smuggles (appearance versus actuality again) diamonds through the customs concealed in plaster saints and rosary beads. Sir Edwin Manders, Laurence's father and the head of Manders Figs in Syrup (a canning concern mentioned in Spark's story 'The Black Madonna') is perpetually lost in religious retreat, having 'frequent recourse to monasteries' (p. 227). Sir Edwin's brother Ernest, a homosexual who runs Eleanor Hogarth's ballet school, blackmails Mervyn Hogarth by hinting at his familiarity with the 'affairs of Louisa Jepp' (p. 150). All these characters obsessively pursue their own ends, a situation that enables Caroline to realize 'we've reached the stage where each one discourses upon his private obsessions' (p. 100). Throughout the novel the various figures confront, but do not comfort, one another.

Most dramatically, since it leads to a splendid set-piece representing a struggle for spiritual survival, Caroline is diametrically opposed to Georgina though both are members of the Roman Catholic Church. Caroline is a Catholic convert, Georgina is a cradle Catholic. Caroline is 'thin, angular, sharp, inquiring' (p. 32), Georgina is a bulky woman with 'a colossal bosom' (p. 29). Caroline is occasionally anorexic (so it is established by the priest providing her with food), Georgina always eats heartily and sticks in Caroline's consciousness 'like a lump of food on the chest which will move neither up nor down' (p. 37). Caroline is an intellectual with bookish interests, Georgina is a dogmatist to whom the often invoked 'Our Lady' (pp. 32–3) is a piece of personal property. In order to save her own soul, Caroline has first to rid herself of Georgina Hogg. It is, for Caroline, a spiritual imperative.

In the final chapter of *The Comforters*, Caroline arranges to have a riverside picnic with Laurence on the banks of the Medway where it borders Kent and Sussex. Laurence's mother Lady Helena comes too, bringing Baron Stock and Georgina Hogg. Ominously the sky clouds over and the picnickers hear the sounds of thunder. Through the rain Georgina, having wandered off, is seen on the opposite bank. 'Caroline, be an angel,' says Helena (p. 223), with unconscious symbolism, when she encourages Caroline to rescue Georgina. After Caroline offers her hand, Georgina slips and pulls her into the water. The two women struggle, as Georgina cannot swim. Spark says of Caroline, choosing her words for their descriptive and metaphorical impact: 'She knew then that if she could not free herself from Mrs Hogg they would both go under' (p. 225). Caroline swims, Georgina sinks. Caroline is free to write her novel. Free will, so *The Comforters* contends, depends on individual emancipation from the burden of evil supported by others. It is, as a moral conclusion, adamantly individualistic. Salvation, for Caroline Rose, is a private affair, the self-centred solution of a personal problem.

The Comforters spices its 'slick plot' (p. 115) with blackmail, bigamy, diabolism and smuggling, and from these unlikely elements it fashions a fable about the isolation of the creative artist. It unsettles the narrative conventions of the novel by putting irony and parody to dazzling effect. The irony of smuggled diamonds being concealed in plaster saints is at once an amusing and telling comment on the emptiness of commercialized images. In a parody of the happy ending, the reader is treated to the marriage of Louisa Jepp and the baker Webster, her partner in crime; the match is not so much made in heaven in the interests of domestic togetherness as motivated by a mutual desire for secrecy. At every level Spark provides her theme with diverting details so that the authority of appearance is undermined. Considering the Typing Ghost that haunts her imagination, Caroline says, 'there's the typewriter too – that's a symbol, but it *is* a real typewriter' (p. 73). It is part of Spark's artistic strategy to ensure that events function on both literal and symbolic levels; her most naturalistic descriptions are always symbolically suggestive. Spark's fictions are subject to an immense literary cunning. And in the broadly realistic climate of British fiction in the 1950s, *The Comforters* was a strikingly radical book, a flamboyant start to a teasing and powerful fictional career.

*

Spark's second novel, *Robinson* (1958), ostensibly tells a more direct tale than *The Comforters*, but from the start there are various hints that the events unfold in an allegorical dimension. Spark overlays her text with ambiguity to render Robinson (the eponymous island and man) metaphysically as well as physically. Robinson the island – though factually solid in the book and graphically outlined in an accompanying map – is also a 'land-scape of the mind' (*R*, p. 7); similarly, the vividly portrayed character Robinson, the island's owner, is a 'legendary figure [of] near-mythical dimensions' (p. 130). During one moment of super-natural speculation the narrator, January Marlow, tells herself that 'Robinson and his household were a dead woman's dream' (p. 36). At times the effect of the island is Edenic, 'the sun blazing hot, and the mists gentle and frequent' (p. 32) but occasionally it makes an infernal impression on January:

> Sometimes, on the plateau where Robinson's house stood, when the wind was from the north or east, a curious smell of burning would pervade the atmosphere, penetrating the rooms. It was sulphurous. Robinson said it came from a bubbling eruption still lively on the mountain, which he called the Furnace. (p. 67)

41

The dead woman's dream, if we concede the presence of that conceit in the novel, has its nightmarish moments.

Told by January Marlow in the first person, *Robinson* purports to be a polished version of the journal kept by the narrator during her three months on the island of Robinson. January has been advised, by Robinson, to 'Keep to facts. . . . Stick to facts' (pp. 17–18) and she obligingly opens her account by blending her fears with some journalistic facts. On 10 May 1954 a plane, bound for the Azores, has crashed on Robinson's island in the North Atlantic ocean. There are three survivors: January herself; Jimmie Waterford, a tall, friendly, partly Dutch kinsman (second cousin or possibly half-brother) of Robinson's; and Tom Wells, a broad-faced English commercial traveller dealing in Druid emblems. January explains that she is a widow with a son. She is also – like her creator – a 'poet, critic, and general articulator of ideas' (p. 23), and a Catholic convert. With the substitution of widowhood for divorce, it is clear that January is a woman in Spark's position, yet the novel is more than an imaginative autobiography. Precisely because Spark invests the text of *Robinson* with various inter-pretative possibilities it has caused critical confusion. An American critic has read it as a Freudian allegory, with Robinson representing January's super-ego, Jimmie Waterford her ego and Tom Wells her id.[40] An English critic has condemned it as 'the most obscure and the least successful of Mrs Spark's novels' before classifying it as a confessional work on the assumption that the plane crash 'is analogous to Mrs Spark's breakdown [in 1953–4], and the enforced sojourn on the island to her period of recovery and return to health'.[41]

Yet though the first-personal format of Robinson contrasts stylistically with the third-personal technique of *The Comforters*, and the manner seems different, thematically Spark's second novel does not differ drastically from her first, for both deal with the isolation of the individual.

Significantly, January is 'the only woman on the island' (*R*, p. 9) and thus a solitary specimen of her sex. For this reason she is drawn towards the moon, a satellite associated (certainly to a literary woman of January's erudition) with the White Moon Goddess, the feminine Muse. On this island, parts of which have a 'moonish landscape' (p. 63), January reflects that 'the pagan mind runs strong in women at any time'; then, punning on the menstrual meaning of period, she recalls 'how my perceptions during that whole period were touched with a pre-ancestral quality, how there was an enchantment, a primitive blood-force which probably moved us all' (p. 9). January – as a woman, as a sensitive individual – is apart from the others. Though she believes there is 'no such thing as a private morality' (p. 161), she is unable to escape from her isolation, noting 'We were on the same island but in different worlds' (p. 144). The literary allusions in the text reinforce January's sense of solitude. Spark's title harks back to Defoe's *Robinson Crusoe* (1719), whose hero was based on Scotland's Alexander Selkirk, speaker of Cowper's poem beginning 'I am monarch of all I survey, / My right there is none to dispute'; and to Johann David Wyss's *The Swiss Family Robinson* (1812–13), cosily unlike *Robinson*. When Jimmie Waterford casually quotes Donne's *Devotions* (1624) by asserting 'No man is an island', January disagrees with him: 'Some are. Their only ground of meeting is concealed under the sea. If words mean anything, and islands exist, then some people are islands' (p. 22). January, by implication, is one of these insular people.

And if some men are islands, January argues, then some islands are men. Robinson the island is presented anthropomorphically. Held east-upmost, the map of Robinson resembles a human shape with the Headlands as head, the North and South Arms as upper extremities, the North and West Leg as lower limbs. Looked at cartographically Robinson's nineteenth-century Spanish-style stone bungalow, on a plateau a thousand feet above sea-level, is located at the navel of the island. There is a secret tunnel at the heart and a live crater, the Furnace, at the liver. The absence of any obvious anatomical landmark at the crotch of the island, situated vulnerably at Shark Bay, has sexual connotations in an allegorical context. January, the lone woman, is able to notice feminine features on an island – 'moon scenery . . . small craters and gulches and lava caverns' (pp. 32–3) – on which Robinson has settled in his celibacy (which Tom Wells takes as a sign of homosexuality). Like a figure sprawling in the ocean, the island Robinson depends for its survival on the outside world. Robinson, owner of the

43

island he has named after himself, does not grow his own food but relies on a supply of tins brought by the pomegranate boat that comes in August. In terms of arranging an escape from the island and the 'curious isolation' (p. 13) of Robinson, there is nothing to do but wait for the pomegranate boat. On this masculine island of men, January is an unwelcome intruder, an alien creature physiologically associated with blood and swiftly shifting moods. January, psychologically alone on the island, is sexually insulated from Robinson, who is 'not a lady's man' (p. 96) and who tells her to take a raincoat if going for a walk since, alas, the 'weather is a woman in this island' (p. 31). Through a Sparkian paradox, January's solitary nature impinges on the others, especially Robinson, who is (so January concludes) 'positively hostile to the idea of women in general' (p. 29).

Extending her theme of spiritual isolation, Spark portrays Robinson as a man antagonistic not only to earthly women, such as January, but to the central Catholic cult of the Virgin Mary, believing Mariolatry to be on a superstitious par with 'Earth mythology' (p. 80). With a characteristic touch of irony, Spark makes Robinson's middle name a celebration of the cult he detests. Miles Mary Robinson, January discovers, is a man apart, a religious recluse intent on keeping his distance from the unholy trinity who have landed on his island. Robinson has studied for the priesthood before refusing to be ordained just as he was due to become a deacon. Dismissing the widespread worship of the Virgin Mary as an unworthy aberration he has written a book, *The Dangers of Marian Doctrine*, maintaining that the Church has fallen into heresy. He takes exception to January's rosary for he feels that the sight of it will corrupt his adopted son Miguel. He is 'constitutionally afraid of any material manifestation of Grace' (p. 99).

Whereas Georgina Hogg, in *The Comforters*, projected herself as an intimate of Our Lady, Robinson is unable to cope with the dogmatic demands of his True Faith on the subject. Despite their intellectual differences, Georgina and Robinson are alike in that they are both characters contaminated by contact with the Catholic faith. Driven by a passion for privacy, Robinson indulges in an outrageously antisocial gesture, though it is some time before

January understands the import of his act. On 3 July 1954, so January explains at the beginning of the eighth chapter of her journal, Robinson disappears. In the mustard field his blood-stained coat is found, a knife in the pocket. Along paths leading to the Furnace is a trail of blood-stained articles including clothes belonging to Robinson, a handkerchief of January's, a blue silk vest once worn by Jimmie Waterford. Robinson is presumed murdered, and January is held to have a motive, because she has said, on noting the disappearance of her rosary, 'If Robinson has taken it I'll murder him. . . . If I find that he came to my room while I was asleep and took my rosary there will be hell to pay' (*R*, p. 96).

Robinson's disappearance coincides with Spark's development of her novel as a moral fable. In the conspicuous absence of the owner of the island, the three temporary inhabitants of Robinson are plunged into a dilemma as deep as the subterranean secret places on Robinson, for they have to judge each other as creatures capable of killing. January is initially shocked into 'a state [of] stupor' (p. 106), Jimmie Waterford seems to accept the situation philosophically, while Tom Wells – sustained by his false faith, occultism, and by his aptitude for evil – welcomes the crisis. Noting that Jimmie Waterford stands to inherit Robinson's property in the event of his death, Wells blackmails Jimmie into promising him money supposedly for injuries inflicted during an earthquake on the island. Though Jimmie acquiesces in this plot, January refuses to be blackmailed when Wells threatens to accuse her of killing Robinson as part of a plan to marry Jimmie Waterford and share Robinson's inheritance.

January understands that evil can be countered by cunning. Recovering her stolen journal from the foot of Tom Wells's bed she decides to hide it near the South Arm end of the subterranean tunnel at the heart of the island, thus ensuring that she has literary evidence of her honesty. Before she sees the light of day again she has to fight her way out of her dilemma. Retracing her journey through the tunnel she is confronted by Tom Wells, who threatens to stab her. January strikes him, then crawls back through 'the terrible hole' (p. 157), emerging into the mist. The next day, in a symbolic struggle between fairly good and utterly evil, Jimmie Waterford and Tom Wells fight over January until the combat is

45

concluded by the unexpected return of Robinson. Even on an island 'a thousand miles from anywhere' (p. 13) a moral law obtains, as January's experience indicates. This is why, exasperated by Robinson's escapism, she tells him 'I chucked the antinomian pose when I was twenty. There's no such thing as a private morality' (p. 161).

January recognizes in Robinson tendencies she must resist if she is to return home and relate to what passes for reality. Robinson's entirely self-centred moral stance, January appreciates, barely covers 'the well of darkness in [his] character' (p. 164). Because he resents the proximity of uninvited guests, he opts out, leaving a false trail by sacrificing his goat and soaking various articles in its blood. This reminds January of her brother-in-law Ian Brodie, whose idea of a practical joke was to tell a man (Curly Lonsdale, January's other brother-in-law) that his wife had cancer of the womb. Rescued from the island, January returns to Chelsea and to the inconsequential chatter of her sisters and their husbands. Later she learns that Tom Wells has been imprisoned for blackmail and that Robinson, the island, is sinking as a result of volcanic action. She has, reluctantly, learned a moral lesson that the individual cannot entirely evade a collective responsibility, cannot forever ignore the existence of evil. By the end of her journal, that is of the novel, January has come to think of the island as 'a place of the mind . . . an apocryphal island' (p. 174). It is, the last sentence claims, a part of her past that convinces her that 'all things are possible' (p. 175). The final flourish advises the reader to avoid a narrow, literal approach to the novel.

Spark's special skill as a novelist creates a fictional situation taut with artistic tension so that the reader has several interpretative options, none of which need be exhaustive. Thus metaphysical possibilities enrich physical descriptions, various incidents have a symbolic significance, several actions have allegorical overtones. For example, the visionary version of the narrative as a dream is evoked through a series of doubles. Two of the men on the island duplicate figures from January's past. Robinson, the renegade Roman Catholic recluse, resembles Ian Brodie, the unpleasant Roman Catholic doctor married to January's sister Agnes; both men are short-tempered, both are selfish, both are capable of mental cruelty, both are opponents of Mariolatry (Robinson on an intellectual, Brodie on an emotional level). Tom Wells, pornographer and professional pedlar of the occult, resembles Curly Lonsdale, a bookie married to January's sister Julia. The correspondences continue, for Miguel, Robinson's adopted son, has an appeal to January as a surrogate for her own son Brian, while Jimmie Waterford attracts her as a possible marital replacement for her dead husband. Early in the novel January informs the reader that she suffered from concussion after her crash, a condition that recurs with the shock of Robinson's disappearance. It is possible, given these clues, to receive the text as a woman's past distorted in a dream.

Spark also drops into her narrative details that transform the tale into a religious allegory. January, the Catholic convert, mentions 'mortal sin' (*R*, p. 39) and 'the deadly sin of pride' (p. 66). With her biblical background she is not slow to see that the plane carrying her to the Azores has crashed on 'a gentle green hillside' (p. 66) on the island of Robinson. If the reader recalls that a plane is constructed in the shape of a cross, he can also see January, Wells and Waterford as characters collectively crucified on a hillside and then, metaphorically, buried on an island. Of the three, one is a blackmailer capable of killing, another an opportunist seeking a fortune – not exactly the two thieves of the Gospels but companions inflicted on the heroine in an emergency. January, the committed Christian, passes 'various stations' (p. 91) on the trail of the missing Robinson (self-appointed deity of the island) and refers to her eventual escape from the island as 'my return from the dead' (p. 91). According to this scenario January re-enacts the Christian drama through mental agony, a kind of crucifixion, an appeal to an indifferent figure of authority and a return to a world largely unmoved by her experience. I am not suggesting that in order to admit such resonances to her fiction Muriel Spark contrives a precise allegorical programme prior to creating a novel; what is more likely is that her sensibility is so saturated in ritual and symbolism that she inevitably extracts the maximum of meaning from the layers of language at her disposal. The various possibilities of interpretation occur simultaneously, alternatives interlock. On Robinson, after all, all things are possible.

*

As experimental applications of fictional form, Spark's first two novels are remarkably successful at conveying the spiritual isolation of a woman temperamentally tempted to solipsism. Both *The Comforters* and *Robinson* project elements of Spark's own personality on to the page in an inventive manner. *The Comforters* uses a neo-modernistic technique to create a distance between reader and heroine; *Robinson* employs the confidential first-personal tone of the journal to engage the reader in the heroine's highly subjective predicament. Spark's psychological quandary, as embodied in Caroline Rose and January Marlow, is how to live with the tiresome imperfections of other people. Caroline and January both indulge in solipsism: Caroline, who hears voices, thinks of others as grist to her artistic mill; January, who wonders if external actuality is merely a dream, is intolerant of those she encounters on the island and back home in Chelsea. *Memento Mori* (1959), Spark's third novel, and one of her most powerful, extends her range by coming to terms with the problems of other people – especially the old – under metaphysical pressure and in physical distress. Apparently the book was thoroughly researched, for Teresa Walshe, the Nursing Sister to whom the novel is dedicated, provided Spark with essential information on the condition of geriatric patients.[42]

Death, as an unavoidable presence in life, is the inescapable external force in Spark's third fiction, as indeed it is in fact. By making mortality as familiar as a voice on the telephone, Spark puts her principal characters under a sentence of death. The narrator does not, however, dominate the novel as a moralistic judge but hovers as a recording angel, observing human frailties objectively. This narratorial detachment does not prevent Spark from penetrating the thoughts of the fictional participants in the plot. Percy Mannering, the agnostic octogenarian poet, goes to the cremation of his former lover Lisa Brooke (dead at the age of 73 after her second stroke), and responds emotionally to her death in infernal images accessible to Spark:

It came to him as the service began that within a few minutes Lisa's coffin would start sliding down into the furnace, and he saw as in a fiery vision her flame-tinted hair aglow as always,

48

competing with the angry tresses of the fire below. He grinned like an elated wolf and shed tears of human grief as if he were half-beast, half-man, instead of half-poet, half-man. Godfrey [Colston] watched him and thought, 'He must be senile. He has probably lost his faculties.' (*MM*, p. 22)

As an observer, the narrator of *Memento Mori* is as omniscient as the Typing Ghost of *The Comforters*.

Though it displays the narrative twists and thematic intrigue typical of Spark, *Memento Mori* remains faithful to its sombre theme of the fatal fragility of old age. With two exceptions, all the characters are old and increasingly infirm, most definitely 'past their prime' (p. 71). Ironically, the two characters under 60 have to live with old age. Olive Mannering, Percy Mannering's 24-year-old granddaughter, is regularly visited in Chelsea by the old rogue Godfrey Colston (aged 87) before she marries Ronald Sidebottome, a widowed businessman of 79. Eric Colston, Godfrey's son, is, at 56, a novelist unable to outgrow the influence of his aged parents. Married to the 'legendary' (p. 10) novelist Charmian Piper, Godfrey is confident that Eric will never match the achievements of his mother: 'He'll never do as well as Charmian did' (p. 12) is his opinion. As they approach death, Godfrey's comment reveals, the old are often impossibly arrogant.

The sentence of death is stated at the beginning of *Memento Mori* as Spark abruptly announces her theme. Dame Lettie Colston, aged 79, receives her ninth call from a man who reiterates his urgent message: 'Remember you must die' (p. 10). Disturbed by this intrusion into her complacency, she discusses her fears with her brother, Godfrey Colston, who attempts to comfort her at his home in Vicarage Gardens, off Kensington Church Street (an address well known to Spark, who lived at Vicarage Gate in 1949–50). The Colstons' home is possessed by the past: Charmian, an 85-year-old lady of letters, relishes the revival of her once-bright reputation; she finds difficulty in distinguishing Lettie from her old family servant Jean Taylor; she wants news of a war that has been history since 1945; she expresses an interest in the obituaries in *The Times*. Charmian's disturbing dottiness is, to Lettie and Godfrey, a symptom of the advanced years they have in common with her. While Lettie is contending with Charmian the telephone rings at Vicarage Gardens and a male voice leaves a message for Lettie instructing her 'to remember she must die' (p. 13). Eventually that message comes to all the principal elderly characters in the novel and they each react in keeping with their characters.

As the phrase 'Remember that you must die' sounds through the novel like a Wagnerian leitmotif in a macabre melodrama, Spark organizes her material into a series of interlinked episodes with plot and subplot competing for the reader's attention. Having admitted the solo voice of death into domestic settings in her opening chapter, she switches to a chorus of ancient voices to place the dying in a clinical calamity. In the Maud Long Medical Ward are twelve old ladies, including Jean Taylor, formerly companion–maid to Charmian Piper. Though arthritic she is lucid enough to meditate on the meaning of death, desperately preserving her dignity, refusing to complain though 'she was forced to cry out with pain during a long haunted night when the dim ward lamp made the beds into grey-white lumps like terrible bundles of laundry which muttered and snored occasionally' (p. 17). She wonders at Dame Lettie's self-indulgent habit of changing her will to the discomfort of her nephews, she sympathizes with Charmian, who has survived a stroke but given up her grip on reality. With Alec Warner, the 79-year-old gerontologist, she is able to expatiate dispassionately on old age. Moreover, Jean – who became a Catholic convert 'just to please Charmian' (p. 45) – has no illusions about the identity of the anonymous caller. 'In my belief,' Jean tells Dame Lettie, 'the author of the anonymous telephone calls is Death himself, as you might say. . . . If you don't remember Death, Death reminds you to do so' (p. 175).

If the disembodied figure of death dominates the novel from a distance, Spark closes in on her characters to examine the precise details of old age and illness. Going beyond the egocentric atmosphere of *The Comforters* and *Robinson*, she shows herself as a scrupulously accurate observer alert to the hardly human condition of infirmity. After the death of Granny Barnacle, a minor though memorable character, the Maud Long Ward is rearranged to accommodate a new geriatric corner. The newcomers are wheeled in, 'in varying advanced states of senility' (p. 117), and next morning 'most, when they were helped out of bed to stand shakily upheld for a moment by the nurse, wet the floor' (p. 118). Spark leaves the reader in no doubt about the grim reality of bodily atrophy. Visiting Jean Taylor in the Maud Long Ward, Alec Warner approaches Mrs Bean, a new patient aged 99. Spark's description of the old lady is an alarmingly vivid verbal portrait of human helplessness:

> He went to speak to Mrs Bean, tiny among the pillows, her small toothless mouth open like an 'O', her skin stretched thin and white over her bones, her huge eye-sockets and eyes in a fixed infant-like stare, and her sparse white hair short and straggling over her brow. Her head nodded faintly and continuously. If she had not been in a female ward, Alec thought, one might not have been sure whether she was a very old man or a woman. She reminded him of one of his mental patients at Folkestone, an old man who, since 1918, had believed he was God. (p. 169)

Imbedded in that passage is the nugget of information about the mental patient. It is a demonstration of the density of Spark's prose that this casually cited connection turns out to be highly relevant, giving the novel a narrative twist. The reader of Spark's prose must be attentive.

Spark complicates her novel with her usual cunning. Having introduced the theme of death through the mysterious phone-calls and scrutinized the dying, she elaborates the plot with intrigue. Mabel Pettigrew, mentioned in the will of her late employer Lisa Brooke, blackmails Godfrey Colston over his affair with Lisa. As well as blackmail there is bigamy, for Lisa, it transpires, was already married to one Matthew O'Brien when she married Guy Leet, the critic. Lisa's will is thus an issue that impinges on Mabel Pettigrew and Guy Leet and, through them, on the Colstons. To the catalogue of crimes such as blackmail and bigamy is added a robbery that results in murder: Dame Lettie is battered to death, at the age of 81, when she discovers a burglar in her house. Towards the end of the novel it is revealed that Matthew O'Brien, identified as Alec Warner's mental patient at Folkestone, is the legal husband of Lisa Brooke and thus the beneficiary of her will. His death saves the situation for Mabel Pettigrew, who inherits a fortune and goes to live in a hotel in South Kensington.

Memento Mori shows Spark in command of an impressive cast of characters, an artistic advance over her first two novels in that both major and minor characters have depth. Godfrey Colston, former chairman of Colston Breweries, has a fetish for looking at women's stockings and suspenders; to practise this peccadillo he is seen in action paying for his pleasure with Mabel Pettigrew (when she comes to look after Charmian) and Olive Mannering. Granny Barnacle, one of the old women in the Maud Long Ward, is a former seller of evening newspapers, has been in Holloway prison, and is bitchy enough to call Sister Burnstead 'Sister Bastard' (*MM*, p. 43). Before she dies she wakes and shouts out the names of newspapers she once sold. In the evening, when the priest comes, the other patients are aware of his purpose, though 'none . . . had sharp enough ears, even with their hearing-aids, to catch more than an occasional humming sound from his recitations' (p. 115). The poignant humour of the hearing-aids leads to the description, after the death of Granny Barnacle, of the collective character of the ward, which 'lay till morning still and soundless, breathing like one body instead of eleven' (p. 116).

For all her comic touches – like the mock-heroic duel with walking sticks between Guy Leet and the old poet Percy Mannering (p. 191) – Spark never neglects her main theme, stated succinctly by Jean Taylor: 'Being over seventy is like being engaged in a war. All our friends are going or gone and we survive amongst the dead and the dying as on a battlefield' (p. 37). Jean's death is the last to be mentioned in the novel, she alone 'employing her pain to magnify the Lord' (p. 220), eschewing the self-centred anguish of the others. Spark's central concern, then, is still the problem of surpassing the limitations of the self – as Jean seems to do by reaching out for a truth larger than fact or fiction. Most of the characters in *Memento Mori* simply succumb to the physical demands of death, as Spark explains in the first of many closing catalogues that neatly round off her novels: 'Charmian died one morning . . . Godfrey died the same year . . . Guy Leet died at the age of seventy-eight. . . . Janet Sidebottome died of a stroke . . . Chief Inspector Mortimer died suddenly of heart-failure . . . Miss

Valvona went to her rest. Many of the grannies followed her' (pp. 218–20).

*

Using a pessimistic exposition and convoluted subplots, *Memento Mori* is a literary performance of considerable complexity, showing Spark so much in technical control of the fictional conventions that she can bend them to her creative will. With the multi-character manipulation of *Memento Mori* behind her, Spark continued her artistic odyssey by creating an extraordinary character through a method of construction derived from the popular ballad. *The Ballad of Peckham Rye* (1960) is mindful of its title. Metrically we expect a ballad to unfold in couplets or, more often, in quatrains such as those employed by Spark in 'The Ballad of the Fanfarlo':

> 'Oh I am Samuel Cramer,' he said,
> 'Born of a German father
> Who was as pale as my naked bone,
> And a brown Chilean mother.'

But the ballad techniques can also be recast in prose by writers who plunge rapidly into the action, who use conversational contrasts to advance the narrative, and who habitually allude to other-worldly phenomena. *The Ballad of Peckham Rye* develops these devices and Spark draws the reader into her design by opening on an exchange that could be read as a quatrain with identical rhymes:

> 'Get away from here, you dirty swine,' she said.
> 'There's a dirty swine in every man,' he said.
> 'Showing your face round here again,' she said.
> 'Now, Mavis, now, Mavis,' he said.

Spark's is a supernatural ballad and her protagonist, Dougal Douglas, is a peculiarly Scottish devil. Not only is he a graduate of Edinburgh University, but he dances the Highland Fling (*BPR*, p. 59), insists 'I'm fey, I've got Highland blood' (p. 67), uses expressions such as 'a wee greet' (p. 67) and 'What guilty wee consciences you've all got' (p. 127). Like the witch in Burns's 'Tam O'Shanter',

53

Dougal dare not cross running water: 'I don't like crossing the river . . . without my broomstick' (p. 87), he explains. Dougal also has characteristics in common with the diabolic figure in one of the greatest Scottish novels, James Hogg's *The Private Memoirs and Confessions of a Justified Sinner* (1824). Gilmartin, Hogg's devil, has the 'cameleon art of changing [his] appearance'.[43] Similarly, Dougal undergoes a series of metaphorical metamorphoses in Spark's book. Interviewed for the post of human researcher by Mr Druce, managing director of the nylon textile firm of Meadows, Meade & Grindley, Dougal (by altering his posture) 'changed his shape and became a professor . . . leaned forward and became a television interviewer' (p. 16). While dancing at Findlater's Ball-room he seems to change in the frenzy of dancing:

Next, Dougal sat on his haunches and banged a message out on a tom-tom. He sprang up and with the lid on his head was a Chinese coolie eating melancholy rice. He was an ardent cyclist, crouched over handlebars and pedalling uphill with the lid between his knees. He was an old woman with an umbrella; he stood on the upturned edges of the lid and speared fish from his rocking canoe; he was the man at the wheel of a racing car. . . . (p. 60)

Pushing the parallels with the traditional ballad, Spark makes ingeniously novel use of two ballad commonplaces during the murder of Merle Coverdale by Mr Druce. In, for example, the ballad of 'Sir Patrick Spens' (as collected in Walter Scott's *Minstrelsy of the Scottish Border*) the wine is 'blude-red'. Appropriately, then, when offered whisky by Mr Druce, Merle opts for an alternative: 'I'll have a glass of red wine. I feel I need something red, to buck me up' (p. 134). With a narrative twist, Spark makes the murder weapon the corkscrew used to open the bottle of blood-red wine, an equivalent of the little penknife that is the obligatory murder weapon in the ballads. Evidently the texture has been well considered and Spark wants her story to have the swift pace of a traditional ballad, the abrupt action of the oral idiom. In order to renew the ballad tradition she also introduces echoes from the most celebrated modernist poem.

Like the traditional ballads, T. S. Eliot's *The Waste Land* (1922) is a powerful poetic influence on Spark's novel. Merle Coverdale is head of the typing pool of Meadows, Meade & Grindley where Mr Druce is her boss. When Mr Druce visits her, in her flat on Denmark Hill, she clatters dishes in the scullery – a variant on Eliot's typist who 'lights / Her stove, and lays out food in tins'.[44] Eliot's typist waits for her expected guest, 'One of the low on whom assurance sits / As a silk hat on a Bradford millionaire'; Mr Druce, a pompous personage, takes off his hat and hangs it on a peg, thus relieving himself of his everyday sign of assurance. Setting the scene for mechanical sex, Eliot says 'The time is now propitious, as he guesses, / The meal is ended, she is bored and tired'; Spark, preparing a similar scene, notes that Merle and Mr Druce 'did not speak throughout the meal [after which] Merle switched on the television' (*BPR*, p. 53). Eliot's lovely woman paces, post-coitally, about the room alone, 'smoothes her hair with automatic hand, / And puts a record on the gramophone'. After sleeping with Mr Druce, Merle 'went into the scullery and put on the kettle while he put on his trousers and went home to his wife' (p. 54).

From *The Waste Land* too, perhaps, comes Spark's interest in the comical aspects of working-class dialogue. Eliot's pub conversation captures the self-congratulatory yet conspiratorial tone of the proletarian monologue:

> He's been in the army four years, he wants a good time,
> And if you don't give it him, there's others will, I said.
> Oh is there, she said. Something o' that, I said.[45]

Spark's ballad has several such passages. Mavis, mother of Dixie Morse the deserted bride, reworks the opening exchange of the novel in her own words:

> So I went to the door, and lo and behold there he was on the doorstep. He said, 'Hallo, Mavis,' he said. I said, 'You just hop it, you.' He said, 'Can I see Dixie?' I said, 'You certainly can't,' I said. I said, 'You're a dirty swine. You remove yourself,' I said, 'and don't show your face again,' I said. (*BPR*, p. 11)

The dirty swine is Humphrey Place, who, under the malicious influence of Dougal, says no when asked if he will take Dixie to be his wedded wife. This scene appears in the first and last chapters of the book, thus providing a narrative frame for the events that occur in Spark's prose ballad. Spark is well aware that the traditional ballads progress by incremental repetition so that an incident is enlarged in the retelling.

The twin influence of tradition and modernism informs Spark's own detailed depiction of Peckham, an area Spark explored when she took a flat in Camberwell in 1956. Peckham is seen as a world within a world; indeed, as the lyrical flourish that closes the novel affirms, it represents 'another world than this' (p. 143). The inhabitants of this other-worldly place include Mavis, Dixie, the loutish Trevor Lomas, Humphrey Place and the incomer Dougal Douglas of Edinburgh. Spark's Peckham also accommodates the textile manufacturing firms of Meadows, Meade & Grindley and its rival Drover Willis's. Dougal works for both firms, dividing himself (as is the way with sinister figures in Scottish fiction) by going under the name Dougal Douglas at the former and Douglas Dougal at the latter. He claims to be an expert researcher into the human problems of the people of Peckham but, with a super-human capacity for mischief, he actually undermines the authority of his employers by advising employees to take days off as a matter of policy. Dougal plays many roles. As a writer he is ghosting the biography of Maria Cheeseman of Chelsea, a retired actress and singer. At the archaeological excavations near Nunhead, where bodies of nuns have been discovered, he passes himself off as 'an interested archaeologist' (p. 102).

Dougal is thus well placed to do the maximum of damage. He discerns a 'fatal flaw' (*passim*) in individuals he encounters and skilfully brings out the worst in them. He goads Trevor Lomas into violence and eventually does battle with him, using the excavated nuns' bones as weapons (p. 139). He sows the seeds of discontent in Humphrey Place so that he despairs of Dixie's dream, of married bliss in a model bungalow. He deliberately unsettles the already neurotic Mr Weedin, personnel manager of Meadows, Meade & Grindley. He leads Mr Druce into temptation by suggesting he live separately from his frigid wife. In such circum-stances it is hardly surprising that Mr Weedin comes to the conclusion that 'Dougal Douglas is a diabolical agent, if not in fact the Devil' (p. 81). Dougal is not, though, Satan come to plague the world. He is built on a smaller scale than that, being content to work on the already suspect morality of a somewhat unsavoury part of London. If Dougal did not exist (taking Spark's fiction as fact) the people of Peckham would have to invent him; the reader is persuaded that Spark has given Peckham the devil it deserves.

Spark cleverly works supernatural fantasy into the fabric of her story. Taking Merle Coverdale for a walk across the common of the Rye, Dougal leads her to the new Cemetery and takes up a posture:

> Dougal posed like an angel on a grave which had only an insignificant headstone. He posed like an angel-devil, with his hump shoulder and gleaming smile, and his fingers of each hand widespead against the sky. She looked startled. Then she laughed. (p. 30)

Subsequently Dougal tells Humphrey Place, who has a room below Dougal's in Miss Frierne's lodging house on the Rye, that he has an erotic dream in which he features as the Devil. He lets Humphrey feel the bumps on his head, explaining that a plastic surgeon took away the two horns in an operation. When Humphrey asks if he is the Devil, Dougal answers, 'No, oh, no. I'm only supposed to be one of the wicked spirits that wander through the world for the ruin of souls' (p. 77). That is precisely his role in Peckham.

Characteristically complicating her plot with blackmail, robbery and violence – Dougal is blackmailed by a schoolboy, Trevor steals a manuscript from him, Merle Coverdale is murdered by Mr Druce – Spark gives her supernatural tale a naturalistic solidity. Peckham is meticulously portrayed with its pubs, cafés and dance-halls, and the flavour of the 1950s is conveyed through transcripts of current slang:

> 'Got any rock and cha-cha on your list, Tony?'
> 'Rev up to it, son. Groove in.'
> Tony turned, replaced his beer on the top of the piano, and rippled his hands over 'Ramona'.
> 'Go, man, go.'

'Any more of that,' said the barmaid, 'and you go man go outside.'

'Yes, that's what *I* say. Tony's the pops.' (*BPR*, p. 109)

As usual, the division between fact and fiction is blurred, for Dougal fabricates details for the biography he is concocting for Maria Cheeseman, attributing to her experiences he has extracted from others. Miss Frierne, the landlady, tells Dougal a story of the Gordon Highlanders, stationed at Peckham during the First World War. Naturally curious about what the Highlanders wore under the kilt, she went to One Tree Hill with a Highlander who 'took her hand and thrust it under his kilt' (p. 40). Dougal duly works this anecdote into Maria Cheeseman's autobiography and when she complains that he is more inventive than accurate he tells her, 'If you only want to write a straight autobiography you should have got a straight ghost. I'm crooked' (p. 76). The pun makes its own point as, bluntly, does Dougal's crooked shoulder. At the end of the novel it is revealed that after leaving Peckham Dougal 'gathered together the scrap ends of his profligate experience . . . and turned them into a lot of cockeyed books' (p. 142). Like Caroline Rose in *The Comforters*, Dougal could be the author of the novel in which he features, a storyteller within a story.

*

By describing an affair central to *The Ballad of Peckham Rye* as 'a legend' (*BPR*, p. 145) in her first chapter and ending the book on a vision of the Rye looking 'like a cloud of green and gold' (p. 143) Spark appeals primarily to the emotion, rather than the intellect, of the reader. Her prose ballad is an atmospheric work, showing an urban landscape under supernatural pressure. Spark's fifth novel, *The Bachelors* (1960), has more definition, for the characters have clear materialistic motives, and are unable to rejoice in the thought of there being 'another world than this' (to cite the final four words of *The Ballad of Peckham Rye*). In *The Ballad of Peckham Rye* the theme of moral desolation is implicit in the behaviour of characters provoked into action by the interference of a diabolic agent; in *The Bachelors* the characters seem predestined to damnation through their devotion to false faiths. Written rapidly within the space of a year,[46] *The Ballad of Peckham Rye* and *The Bachelors* show Spark's ability to approach a problem – for her the only problem, namely the existence of evil in a world made in the image of a benign God – from strikingly different angles.

The Bachelors is an exposure of the emptiness of spurious religions. In the novel there are three false faiths, beginning with bachelordom itself. Three of the characters, the narrator explains, 'were bachelors of varying degrees of confirmation' (*B*, p. 19), while Ronald Bridges, the graphologist, insists 'I'm a *confirmed* bachelor' (p. 77) and observes that but for a development in human nature 'spinsters and bachelors would all be in religious orders' (p. 78). Ronald, indeed, had once aspired to the Roman Catholic priesthood but abandoned this calling when visited by the misfortune of epilepsy. Ronald's egregiously false faith of bachelordom – involving a solipsism of the spirit – has pyschological as well as physical consequences. Thinking of his early epileptic experiences he feels himself to be 'one possessed by a demon' (p. 14).

In the context of the novel, the 'ridiculous demons' (p. 108) who possess Ronald are the other characters. They too live their lives by false faiths. Patrick Seton, the 55-year-old medium, is a spiritualist as well as a bachelor. He is Ronald's opposite number in the novel, a bachelor of criminal cunning, whereas Ronald is a bachelor of professional competence. Both seem to be demoniacally possessed. When Patrick goes into a trance he is transformed: 'Then his eyes opened and turned upward in their sockets. Foam began to bubble at his mouth and faintly trickled down his chin' (p. 36). Ronald, in the grip of an epileptic fit, manifests identical symptoms: 'he foamed at the mouth [and] his eyes turned upward' (p. 198). Though both men have had intimations of 'another world than this' (Patrick through his spiritualist talents, Ronald through his priestly past) they renounce it and are therefore vulnerable to the everyday evil which Spark discerns in the world.

Patrick Seton practises his spiritualism with the Wider Infinity, a group with headquarters in Marlene Cooper's flat in Bayswater. Able to impress gullible women, Patrick takes advantage of them.

At the outset of the story Martin Bowles, the barrister, tells Ronald that Patrick Seton is about to face a charge of fraudulent conversion as he has forged a letter cheating the widow Freda Flower out of two thousand pounds. Moreover, Patrick has convinced Alice Dawes, his pregnant mistress, that he intends to marry her whereas he actually plans to murder her by overdosing her with insulin, she being a diabetic. Completing his catalogue of crimes, Patrick blackmails Dr Lyte, obtaining drugs and money in return for keeping the doctor's secret about an illegal, and fatal, operation.

In addition to bachelordom and spiritualism, the third of the false faiths in *The Bachelors* is homosexuality. Elsie Forrest – Alice Dawes's friend and fellow-worker in the Oriflamme coffee-bar in Kensington – does some typing for Father Socket, a spiritualist clergyman. Elsie steals, from Ronald Bridges, a letter forged by Patrick Seton. Intending to place this incriminating epistle in Socket's hands she visits him and is aghast when the door is opened by Mike Garland, a homosexual. Elsie, a highly sexed woman, is 'very put out, especially by Mike's lipstick' (*B*, p. 123), and resolves to retain the letter. Subsequently Spark explains that for Mike Garland, a former inmate of Maidstone prison, homosexuality is a faith blessed by Father Socket:

> Father Socket had . . . bestowed larger thoughts on Mike, who began to experience a late flowering in his soul. Father Socket cited the classics and André Gide, and although Mike did not actually read them, he understood, for the first time in his life, that the world contained scriptures to support his homosexuality which, till now, had been shifty and creedless. . . . Mike felt secure with Father Socket [for he] was no longer an aimless chancer sliding in and out of illegal avenues, feeling resentful all the while. Mike now was at rights with the world, he was somebody. He had a religion and a Way of Life, set forth by Father Socket. (pp. 150–1)

Once a common criminal, Mike has become – thanks to Father Socket – a man with a profound faith in his own homosexual nature.

With heavy irony, Spark reveals the flimsy foundations of the three spurious religions. The bachelor Martin Bowles, counsel for

the prosecution in the court case against Patrick Seton for fraudulent conversion, is himself involved in cheating a gullible woman
out of her money. Martin has obtained forty thousand pounds
from the divorcée Isobel Billows, which is twenty times more than
Patrick Seton has extracted from the widow Freda Flower. Putting
his arm round Isobel, Martin tells her, 'You must be protected
from spongers' (p. 136), an ironic statement for a skilled sponger
to make. In the court case, Ronald's reflections on Martin's
duplicity provide a commentary on the irony of the situation.
After having an epileptic fit in court, Ronald watches Martin
condemn Patrick before the jury:

> 'He [Martin refers to Patrick Seton] did not hesitate to rob
> her, he did not hesitate to exert his influence by means of those
> intimate relations with Mrs Flower.'
> With Isobel Billows, thought Ronald.
> 'And yet he stands here and poses as her protector. You
> observe the irony, ladies and gentlemen of the jury.'
> The irony, ladies and gentlemen, thought Ronald. (p. 210)

Ronald's silent acceptance of Martin's iniquity constitutes his
small sin. He is the hero of the novel in a limited sense, only
comparatively decent.

The novel weaves its plot around a collection of lost souls at sea
in London, 'the great city of bachelors' (p. 7). Ronald has missed
his priestly vocation, Patrick Seton has abused his impressive
powers as a medium, Martin Bowles has betrayed the declared
standards of the legal profession, Dr Lyte has fallen from medical
grace, Father Socket has exploited the sexual weakness of his
associates, Elsie Forrest has shown a willingness to sell her soul for
sexual gratification. They are all, in various degrees, frauds. Spark
dwells on the moral vacuity of her characters in two spectacular
set-pieces. First, there is the séance at which Patrick goes into a
trance (pp. 34–40); counterpointing this event is the trial (chapter
12), at which the main characters make asses of themselves in the
eyes of the law. Eventually, Patrick Seton is sentenced to five years'
imprisonment and Ronald attempts to 'walk off his demons' (p.
214), realizing that Patrick, Martin, Socket and the others are
'fruitless souls, crumbling tinder, like his own self which did not

bear thinking of' (p. 214). He knows that while Patrick has been sent to jail, Martin – Patrick's accuser – is at large to continue to cheat Isobel Billows. He knows, too, that Matthew Finch, the Jesuit-trained London correspondent of the *Irish Echo*, will marry Alice, pregnant by Patrick Seton. All Ronald has learned from life is an awareness of evil:

> It is all demonology and to do with creatures of the air, and there are others beside ourselves, he thought, who lie in their beds like happy countries that have no history. Others ferment in prison; some rot, maimed; some lean over the banisters of presbyteries to see if anyone is going to answer the telephone. (p. 214)

Ronald is alone, a Catholic corrupted by the false faith of bachelordom, a graphologist unable to read the spiritual messages that surround him.

3

JEAN BRODIE, THE GIRLS, THE GATE

Several of Muriel Spark's novels place characters in insulated areas, contain them in tightly knit communities: the pilgrim centre in *The Comforters* (1957), the island in *Robinson* (1958), the geriatric ward in *Memento Mori* (1959), the hostel in *The Girls of Slender Means* (1963), the big house in *Not to Disturb* (1971), the apartment in *The Hothouse by the East River* (1973), the convent in *The Abbess of Crewe* (1974). Nowhere in Spark's output is the microcosmic world-within-a-world scenario more skilfully realized than in *The Prime of Miss Jean Brodie* (1961), arguably her masterpiece. Rapidly written in eight weeks,[47] the novel is set in and around an Edinburgh girls' school – Marcia Blaine, modelled on James Gillespie's, where Spark was educated – and has for its heroine a woman physically vibrant with vitality, assuredly in her prime.

Jean Brodie is one of the great character-creations of modern fiction, a contradictory soul who distrusts the Roman Catholic Church while spending summer holidays in Rome in search of culture; who admires the Church of Scotland but detests John Knox, its founder; who deplores the team spirit yet idolizes Mussolini's fascisti; who articulates a doctrine of romantic love yet sleeps with the dreary Mr Lowther and denies herself to one-armed Mr Lloyd because he is a married man with children. Though the central part of an accomplished fiction, Jean Brodie seems undeniably real, and Spark's friend Derek Stanford claims to have been 'introduced to the original of that audacious teacher by Muriel at the Poetry Society'.[48] Spark herself has stated 'there was no "real" Miss Brodie,'[49] and 'there was a Christina Kay who died during the '40s, greatly esteemed, but not like Miss Brodie in character.'[50] Jean Brodie may be a fact of fiction rather than life (the distinction between the two being blurred by Sparkian metaphysics) but then so are all Spark's characters: the difference between Jean Brodie and the others is that she appears to have an actual existence over and above the pages of a book that operates by implication. This is why she has been successfully transferred to stage, cinema and television. For thousands of readers, Jean Brodie actually exists in the same way that Sherlock Holmes and George Smiley actually exist.[51] Though no saint, Jean Brodie is a literary legend.

The author's affection for Jean Brodie and her native city gives this novel of the 1930s a period charm that is rare in the caustic Spark canon. For *The Prime of Miss Jean Brodie* Spark has reserved some of her most richly lyrical prose. The novel abounds in evocative phrases: 'the haunted November twilight of Edinburgh' (*PMJB*, p. 20), 'The evening paper rattle-snaked its way through the letter box and there was suddenly a six-o'clock feeling in the house' (p. 21), 'Miss Brodie's voice soared up to the ceiling, and curled round the feet of the Senior girls upstairs' (pp. 21–2), 'The bare winter top branches of the trees brushed the windows of this long [science] room, and beyond that was the cold winter sky with a huge red sun' (p. 24), 'The wind blew from the icy Forth and the sky was loaded with forthcoming snow' (p. 27), 'Miss Brodie, indifferent to criticism as a crag' (p. 60), 'Her name and memory, after her death, flitted from mouth to mouth like swallows in summer, and in winter they were gone' (p. 127). Several of these poetic phrases make the novel, on one level, an elegy for an Edinburgh that has gone, though it lingers in the memory of Muriel Spark. Edinburgh, the home of Jean Brodie, is also identified by Spark as the city where John Knox clashed with Mary Queen of Scots; where Jean Brodie's ancestor Deacon Brodie (the original of Stevenson's dualistic Dr Jekyll) roamed as a burgher by day and a burglar by night; where spinsters such as Jean Brodie 'called themselves Europeans and Edinburgh a European capital, the city of Hume and Boswell' (p. 43). Haunted by its historic past and pressurized by the 'progressive spinsters of

Edinburgh' (p. 42), the city acquires a magical dimension: 'dark heavy Edinburgh itself could suddenly be changed into a floating city when the light was a special pearly white and fell upon one of the gracefully fashioned streets' (p. 111).

The contradictions in Jean Brodie's character are partly explained by the contrasts apparent in Edinburgh. On a long winter's walk in 1930, during which Sandy Stranger comes to the conclusion that 'the Brodie set was Miss Brodie's fascisti' (p. 31), the girls are taken from the classically proportioned New Town to the 'reeking network of slums which the Old Town constituted in those years' (p. 32). The Old Town is another world-within-a world (or town-within-a-city), a no-girl's-land that has the alien atmosphere of a foreign country. Miss Brodie leads her privileged girls into the unpromising land of the Grassmarket:

A man sat on the icy-cold pavement; he just sat. A crowd of children, some without shoes, were playing some fight game, and some boys shouted after Miss Brodie's violet-clad company, with words that the girls had not heard before, but rightly understood to be obscene. Children and women with shawls came in and out of the dark closes. . . . A man and a woman stood in the midst of the crowd which had formed a ring round them. They were shouting at each other and the man hit the woman twice across the head. (pp. 32–3)

In such a city, with its internal and eternal dichotomies, reality has several strata and a woman such as Jean Brodie can be in two minds at once. Like many Scots, Jean Brodie has a divided self.

Theologically, Jean Brodie's Edinburgh – where schoolteachers bid their good mornings 'with predestination in their smiles' (p. 75) – is a place fashioned by John Knox from the philosophy of Calvin. Sandy Stranger, half-English, recognizes that the bleak doctrine of the elect is built into Edinburgh where elegance coexists with squalor. 'In fact,' Spark declares, 'it was the religion of Calvin of which Sandy felt deprived, or rather a specified recognition of it. She desired this birthright; something definite to reject' (p. 108). Increasingly, Sandy Stranger makes a connection between Jean Brodie's scholastic élite and John Calvin's elect. The insight causes her to lose faith in her teacher:

she began to sense what went to the makings of Miss Brodie
who had elected herself to grace in so particular a way and with
more exotic suicidal enchantment than if she had simply taken
to drink like other spinsters who couldn't stand it any more.
(p. 109)

If *The Prime of Miss Jean Brodie* is constructed around a microcosmic notion, it is not imaginatively limited by its location:
behind the (albeit fictional) reality of Miss Brodie there are the
historical figures of Knox, Calvin, Mussolini, Franco and Hitler.
Spark's novel is enormously suggestive: the account of a group of
schoolgirls and their teacher is also a statement on the nature of
faith and fanaticism.

Jean Brodie's prime is officially launched in 1930, when the
heroine is 39. A teacher in the Junior department of Marcia Blaine
School, she chooses for her disciples (the biblical subtext is
evident) six 10-year-old girls: Monica Douglas, who is famous for
mathematics and subsequently marries a scientist; Rose Stanley,
famous for sex, who marries a businessman; Eunice Gardiner,
famous for gymnastics, who becomes a nurse married to a doctor;
Mary Macgregor, famous for being 'a silent lump, a nobody'
(*PMJB*, p. 8), who dies in a fire at the age of 23; Jenny Gray,
famous for being pretty, who becomes an actress; and Sandy
Stranger, 'notorious for her small, almost non-existent, eyes' (p.
7), who becomes a nun famous for her psychological treatise, 'The
Transfiguration of the Commonplace'. Sandy, the future Sister
Helena of the Transfiguration, Jean Brodie's darling disciple, is
the Judas who betrays her teacher to the headmistress, Miss
Mackay. As a result Miss Brodie is forced to retire in 1939, the
year of a new world war, for teaching fascism – especially to Joyce
Emily Hammond, who dies on her way to fight for Franco at Miss
Brodie's bidding.

Technically, the novel is told in a series of flashbacks and
flashforwards. It opens in 1936, breaks back to 1930 (the first year
of Miss Brodie's prime) then uses timeshifts to indicate the rise of
the Brodie set and the fall of Miss Brodie. Before the final tale of
Miss Brodie's downfall has been told, the reader is given the date
of the heroine's death: in 1946, at the age of 55, after 'suffering

from an internal growth' (p. 56). In *The Comforters* Spark queried the concept of authorial omniscience; in *The Prime of Miss Jean Brodie* she makes full use of it, magisterially providing the reader with the information she explores in the novel. She also delivers herself of a personal opinion as if her heroine were an actual rather than a fictional woman:

> In some ways, her attitude [of hostility to Roman Catholicism] was a strange one, because she was by temperament suited only to the Roman Catholic Church; possibly it could have embraced, even while it disciplined, her soaring and diving spirit, it might even have normalized her. (p. 85)

The comment encourages the reader to believe in the reality of Jean Brodie, appropriately so since she is Spark's most forgivable character.

For all her admiration of her heroine, Spark makes fun of her fantasies. There is a reductive, comic quality to Jean Brodie's assumption of the leadership of an élite corps of schoolgirls. An admirer of Il Duce, Mussolini, she defines teaching as 'a leading out, from *e*, out and *duco*, I lead' (p. 45). Regarding her pupils as the 'crème de la crème' (p. 8) she indoctrinates her élite – her elect – with her own prejudices. Her pupils are 'vastly informed on a lot of subjects irrelevant to the authorized curriculum' (p. 5), being familiar with the accomplishments of Sybil Thorndike and Anna Pavlova and, above all, with the romantic tale of Jean's lover, Hugh Carruthers, who fell 'like an autumn leaf' (p. 12) – so she informs the girls in autumn under an elm – at Flanders, a tragedy enlarged with frequent retellings. Like her heroes – Mussolini, Franco, Hitler – Miss Brodie is a dogmatist. When she asks her class to name the greatest Italian painter and one pupil names Leonardo da Vinci, she says, revealingly, 'That is incorrect. The answer is Giotto, he is my favourite' (p. 11). In place of observations, she inflicts on the girls her dogmatic assertions: 'Art is greater than science' (p. 25), 'Mussolini is one of the greatest men in the world' (p. 44), and (preposterously) 'unemployment is even farther abolished under [Mussolini] than it was last year' (p. 45).

Projecting herself as the peer of fascist dictators, Jean Brodie nevertheless remains the victim of her own urban and intellectual environment, 'for in many ways Miss Brodie was an Edinburgh spinster of the deepest dye' (p. 26). Like other Spark heroines she is inclined to solipsism, unable to understand the wider world except as an extension of herself. If circumstances do not accommodate her expectations she attempts to satisfy her desires deviously. Teddy Lloyd, the art teacher, is a married man, which means that she can only allow herself to kiss him surreptitiously in the art room, a gesture she believes preserves her personal purity. Arrogantly, however, she decides to make love to Teddy vicariously by sacrificing one of her girls, choosing Rose Stanley to be her surrogate. Convinced that the girls only exist to do her will, she feels she can thus have the best of both worlds: the world of the Edinburgh spinster as well as the world of the romantic heroine. In the event, it is Sandy Stranger, not Rose Stanley, who sleeps with Teddy Lloyd. The art teacher accepts the substitute physically but remains besotted by Jean: all his portraits of the Brodie set reproduce her features on their faces. Miss Brodie's physical affair with Mr Lowther, the music teacher, is also rationalized, for she sleeps with this bachelor 'in a spirit of definite duty, if not exactly martyrdom' (p. 86). Tragically, Jean's hypocrisy leads to the loss of everything that is precious to her: the friendship of Mr Lowther (who marries the science teacher), the devotion of Teddy Lloyd, the position she holds at Marcia Blaine, the adoration of her girls.

Surely no girls in adult fiction have ever been portrayed so unsentimentally as the Brodie set. Sandy Stranger and Jenny Gray are obsessed with sex from the age of 10. Thinking of Miss Brodie's prime, they see her belonging to a different species from their parents. 'They don't have primes,' says Sandy. 'They have sexual intercourse,' adds Jenny (*PMJB*, p. 16). Sandy, who has fantasies about the heroes of *Kidnapped* and *Jane Eyre*, is reduced to giggles when Mr Lloyd shows lantern slides of Italian paintings and points at the curves on Botticelli's female figures. Sandy and Jenny giggle together over the lewd mechanics of sewing-machines. Between them Sandy and Jenny concoct a romantic fiction around Jean Brodie's supposed sexual adventures with Hugh of Flanders Field and Mr Lowther. This subplot allows Spark to parody romantic pulp-fiction with glorious comic results, culminating in a letter the girls imagine Miss Brodie writing to Gordon Lowther:

> Your letter has moved me deeply as you may imagine [but] there is another in my life whose mutual love reaches out to me beyond the bounds of Time and Space. He is Teddy Lloyd! Intimacy has never taken place with him. He is married to another. One day in the art room we melted into each other's arms and knew the truth. But I was proud of giving myself to you when you came and took me in the bracken on Arthur's Seat while the storm raged about us. . . . I may permit misconduct to occur again from time to time as an outlet because I am in my Prime. . . . Allow me, in conclusion, to congratulate you warmly upon your sexual intercourse, as well as your singing. (pp. 73–4)

When Jenny sees a man exposing himself beside the Water of Leith, Sandy is transported into a Walter Mitty world in which she befriends the policewoman (suitably romanticized) who had questioned Jenny. By the time they are 12 the two girls feel they have, imaginatively, done it all:

> The world of pure sex seemed years away. Jenny had turned twelve. Her mother had recently given birth to a baby boy, and the event had not moved them even to speculate upon its origin.
>
> 'There's not much time for sex research in the Senior school,' Sandy said.
>
> 'I feel I'm past it,' said Jenny. (p. 80)

Linguistically *The Prime of Miss Jean Brodie* is a treat. Spark's use of cross-references, for example, creates irony. Eunice Gardiner is reprimanded by Miss Brodie for using the adjective 'social' as a noun (p. 62). The incident connects with a flashforward, early in the novel, when Eunice, a married woman, tells her husband she wishes to go and visit Miss Brodie's grave:

> 'Who was Miss Brodie?'
>
> 'A teacher of mine, she was full of culture. She was an Edinburgh Festival all on her own. She used to give us teas at her flat and tell us about her prime.'
>
> 'Prime what?' (p. 27)

Elsewhere Spark's dialogue provides exquisite comic exchanges. Monica Douglas's claim that she has seen Teddy Lloyd kissing Miss Brodie in the art room is queried by Sandy Stranger:

> 'What part of the art room were they standing in?' Sandy said.
> 'The far side,' Monica said. 'I know he had his arm round her and was kissing her. They jumped apart when I opened the door.'
> 'Which arm?' Sandy snapped.
> 'The right of course, he hasn't got a left.' (p. 51)

The interrogation continues:

> 'Was it a long and lingering kiss?' Sandy demanded, while Jenny came close to hear the answer.
> Monica cast the corner of her eye up to the ceiling as if doing mental arithmetic. Then when her calculation was finished she said, 'Yes it was.'
> 'How do you know if you didn't stop to see how long it was?'
> 'I know,' said Monica, getting angry, 'by the bit that I did see. It was a small bit of a good long kiss that I saw, I could tell it by his arm being round her.' (pp. 51–2)

Using a descriptive device, Spark attaches to the principal characters a set of words that stick to them throughout the novel. Jean Brodie is forever proclaiming her prime, Sandy Stranger is constantly condemned by her eyes – her 'small, almost non-existent eyes' (p. 7), 'her little eyes screwed on Miss Brodie' (p. 22), 'a hypocritical blinking of her eyes' (p. 50), 'her little pig-like eyes' (p. 66), her 'abnormally small eyes' (p. 124). Teddy Lloyd first kisses Sandy because of her eyes, telling her 'That'll teach you to look at an artist like that' (p. 102). Mary Macgregor's presence in the novel is verbally linked to death by fire. The manner of her death is described at the beginning of the second chapter of the novel:

> [After the outbreak of the Second World War, Mary] died while on leave in Cumberland in a fire in the hotel. Back and forth along the corridors ran Mary Macgregor, through the thickening smoke. She ran one way; then, turning, the other way; and at either end the blast furnace of the fire met her. (p. 15)

Shortly after this flashforward there is an allusion to Mary 'who later, in that hotel fire, ran hither and thither till she died' (p. 28). Armed with this foreknowledge, the reader is then alerted to the significance of Mary's panic as a schoolgirl during an experiment in the science room when magnesium flares shoot out of test-tubes:

> Mary Macgregor took fright and ran along a single lane between two benches, met with a white flame, and ran back to meet another brilliant tongue of fire. Hither and thither she ran in panic between the benches until she was caught and induced to calm down. (p. 76)

The prose here has the poetic force of a refrain and in such ways Spark conditions the reader's responses to various situations in the novel.

Thematically, *The Prime of Miss Jean Brodie* is a persuasive study of the élitist mentality that powers the body of the heroine. 'Give me a girl at an impressionable age, and she is mine for life' (p. 9), says Miss Brodie, but Sandy Stranger, the most reflective of the disciples, realizes that her leader is flawed by fanaticism. Ironically, Sandy's own fantasies are flattened by the sexual facts of life and she retreats from Miss Brodie, who is suddenly seen as ridiculous rather than sublime. After ruining Miss Brodie's teaching career, Sandy retreats further from everyday reality, not into a school but into the Catholic Church, 'in whose ranks she had found quite a number of Fascists much less agreeable than Miss Brodie' (p. 125). It is Sandy Stranger, alias Sister Helena of the Transfiguration, who delivers the last words in the book, from the isolation of her nunnery. Asked about the main influences in her life Sandy says 'there was a Miss Jean Brodie in her prime' (p. 127). The commonplace has been transfigured: Sandy's life, like the reader's, has been enriched by the charismatic personality of Jean Brodie, who, for all her faults, has a poetic panache.

*

The magnificent opening paragraph of *The Girls of Slender Means* (1963) shows how Spark can peel back layer after layer of meaning when she observes with what she calls, in her poem

'Elementary', her 'odd capacity for vision'. Majestically she begins with a fairy-tale format and ends on a metaphysical assumption:

> Long ago in 1945 all the nice people in England were poor, allowing for exceptions. The streets of the cities were lined with buildings in bad repair or in no repair at all, bomb-sites piled with stony rubble, houses like giant teeth in which decay had been drilled out, leaving only the cavity. Some bomb-ripped buildings looked like the ruins of ancient castles until, at a closer view, the wallpapers of various quite normal rooms would be visible, room above room, exposed, as on a stage, with one wall missing; sometimes a lavatory chain would dangle over nothing from a fourth- or fifth-floor ceiling; most of all the staircases survived, like a new art-form, leading up and up to an un-specified destination that made unusual demands on the mind's eye. All the nice people were poor; at least, that was a general axiom, the best of the rich being poor in spirit. (*GSM*, p. 7)

As that passage indicates, Spark is an artist who imposes form on her material. The scene is not simply depicted, it is transformed by linguistic means. There are striking similes – 'like giant teeth . . . like the ruins of ancient castles . . . like a new art-form' – and authorial opinions. It is evident that Spark herself is making 'unusual demands on the mind's eye'; she confronts realistic detail with surrealistic tension, invests natural objects with supernatural associations (those bomb-ripped buildings with their Gothic contours).

Spark enjoys telling tales about characters who seem frozen in the narrative past. *The Girls of Slender Means* begins and ends with the fairy-tale phrase 'long ago in 1945', which establishes a sense of temporal distance from the narrative present, established in a series of phone-calls made by Jane Wright, a gossip columnist. Jane phones Dorothy Markham, owner of a model agency; Anne Baberton, a busy housewife, domesticated with children; Rudi Bittesch, a Rumanian dealer in books and manuscripts; Pauline Fox, a woman receiving psychiatric treatment; Lady Julia Markham, an officious aristocrat; and Nancy Riddle, a clergy-man's wife. The information she imparts to these characters has been gathered by Jane from a news paragraph from Reuters. Nicholas Farringdon, a missionary and former poet, has been killed, 'Martyred in Haiti' (p. 10).

Each acquaintance treats Jane's information about Nicholas with indifference, each wishing to bury the past that pulsates through Spark's novel. It is thus impressed on the reader that the narrative facts of Spark's modern fairy tale may be controversial. Spark places a private text carefully within a public context, inviting a comparison between the intimate and the epic. She makes several references to great global issues: the Allied victory over Germany, the explosion of the atomic bomb over Hiroshima, the Allied victory over Japan. London, a city affected by such events, alternates between grim realities and great expectations, for food-rationing continues and Labour replaces the Conservative government. Against such a background unfolds the story of the girls of slender means who inhabit a world within a world within a world. To Nicholas Farringdon, the May of Teck Club, which accommodates the girls, is 'a miniature expression of a free society . . . a community held together by the graceful attributes of a common poverty' (pp. 84–5). Spark is, of course, an ironist.

Standing obliquely opposite the site of the Albert Memorial, the May of Teck Club is a spacious part of a row of tall houses overlooking Kensington Gardens. Named after the Princess May of Teck (as Queen Mary was called before her marriage to George V) the club exists, as the Edwardian constitution makes clear, 'for the Pecuniary Convenience and Social Protection of Ladies of Slender Means below the age of Thirty Years, who are obliged to reside apart from their Families in order to follow an Occupation in London' (p. 19). The Victorian house, in which the girls live, is projected as a haven against the hardships of the world. Before she investigates the actuality behind the appearance, Spark describes the girls' domestic environment in detail.

In the basement of the hostel – though no one refers to it as a hostel 'except in moments of low personal morale' (p. 26) – are kitchens, laundry, furnace and fuel-stores. On the first floor is an enormous dormitory for the youngest members of the Club and above that staff quarters and shared bedrooms. The third floor is the domain of three old maids (Collie, Jarvie, Greggie); mad

Pauline Fox with her fantasies of dining with the actor Jack Buchanan; and Joanna Childe, the rector's daughter, who teaches elocution through the articulation of her favourite poems. At the top of the house, on the fourth floor, the five most beautiful and sophisticated girls have their rooms: Selina Redwood, 'exceedingly beautiful [and] extremely slim' (pp. 31–2), Anne Baberton, 'slender and already fixed up for marriage' (p. 33), Dorothy Markham, whose 'hips were thirty-six and a half inches' (p. 43), Nancy Riddle, a clergyman's daughter intent on eliminating her Midlands accent by taking elocution lessons from Joanna; and Jane Wright, 'who was miserable about her fatness and spent much of her time in eager dread of the next meal' (p. 32).

The dimensions of the girls are psychologically and physically important. With their slender financial means they cannot afford ethical absolutes, so ration their moral resources. Three of the top-floor girls, for instance, have lovers 'in addition to men-friends with whom they did not sleep but whom they cultivated with a view to marriage' (p. 30). Slender proportions are essential, too, in providing a release from the Club. For above the fourth floor there are the roof-tops, with a portion of flat roof suitable for sun-bathing. As access to this is through a lavatory window measuring 7 inches by 14 inches, only the slimmest girls can squeeze through it. Selina easily passes through the aperture while Anne Baberton can do it naked and Dorothy Markham manages to push her 'hipless and breastless shape' (p. 44) past the 'narrow slit' (p. 32). The girls' proportions are a slender means towards a literary end, for, when a bomb explodes in the garden and fire breaks out in the house, fourteen females remain in the upper storeys. Selina, Anne and Pauline Fox slip through the window, others – including Jane Wright – are rescued when firemen open an old bricked-up skylight. Joanna Childe, however, dies when the house collapses around her.

There are memorable symbolic moments in that climactic scene of fire and explosion. Throughout the book Spark's descriptive prose has been punctuated by the poetry recited by Joanna, whose great set-piece is Hopkins's 'The Wreck of the Deutschland'. It is, therefore, ironically apt that Joanna, with her self-consciously poetic presence, should be the one piece of human wreckage when

74

the Kensington house is wrecked by a German bomb. Before she dies, though, Joanna makes a gesture appropriate to the irrational situation. As it is known in the Club that thirty-six and a quarter inches is the maximum size for hips that can squeeze through the lavatory window, Joanna finds a tape-measure and attempts to size up the trapped girls: 'Joanna's efforts to measure them had been like a scientific ritual in a hopeless case, it had been a something done, it provided a slightly calming distraction' (p. 123).

Selina Redwood, the slender girl who easily slips through the lavatory window, makes a more selfish gesture, though it is fraught with danger. Having extricated herself from the lavatory, Selina goes back into the burning house. It is not immediately apparent why she has returned, though Nicholas Farringdon, observing the situation from the roof, erroneously assumes she has gone back to rescue one of the girls. Not so. Earlier in the novel much has been made of the Schiaparelli taffeta evening dress owned by Anne Baberton and lent out by her, in exchange for extra rations, to the other top-floor girls. Selina, on her return to the smoke-filled house, is seen carrying 'something fairly long and limp and evidently light in weight, enfolding it carefully in her arms [and] Nicholas thought it was a body' (p. 125). It is the Schiaparelli dress. Even as her little world crumbles, Selina has her own priorities. She is the most self-centred of all the girls.

Gestures are crucial to *The Girls of Slender Means*, for Nicholas Farringdon, bisexual poet and anarchist, is altered by them. He brings to the girls in general the bohemian habits of Fitzrovia (where he frequents the Wheatsheaf and the Gargoyle); to Jane, in particular, he brings *The Sabbath Notebooks*, a pseudo-profound treatise which he hopes she will promote in her capacity as publisher's assistant. What he actually achieves is access to the Club's roof, through the top floor of the hotel next door, so that he can make love to Selina on the roof. When Selina emerges safely from the fire at the Club he makes 'an entirely unaccustomed gesture, the signing of the cross upon himself' (p. 60). Subsequently, when he sees a seaman murder a woman he thrusts a document down the killer's blouse 'for no apparent reason and to no effect, except that it was a gesture' (p. 141). Spark acknowledges the grace of certain gestures but insinuates that gestures are not enough. Nicholas, whose death is sounded through the novel like a memento mori, dies making the hopeless gesture of attempting to convert the Haitians.

The finale of the book suggests that global gestures, too, are insufficient. During the public celebrations for Victory in Japan night, Jane, Nicholas and Rudi Bittesch are caught in the crush of the ecstatic crowd. After Nicholas sees the seaman stab a woman, the three companions witness a fight between British and American servicemen. The victory over Japan contains its own contradictions, as Spark's ironical use of allusion demonstrates: 'Two men lay unconscious at the side of the path, being tended by their friends. The crowds cheered in the distance behind them. A formation of aircraft buzzed across the night sky. It was a glorious victory' (p. 142). The final phrase echoes Robert Southey's poem 'The Battle of Blenheim' (1798), which sardonically reiterates the refrain 'It was a famous victory'.

Spark's closing scene harks back to the Victory in Europe celebrations at the beginning of the book when the surge of the crowd dissolves into a sea of promiscuity. The verbal group-portrait of the girls of slender means is thus framed by a grand construction signifying the bigger world beyond the May of Teck Club: bigger, but not conspicuously better. The story of the girls is both specific and symbolic; events in their lives seem to imply a cosmic catastrophe. The bomb that explodes in the garden and sets fire to the May of Teck Club is a small blast in an explosive world. Spark clarifies this symbolism by counter-pointing the Kensington fire against an image of the world beyond:

when in London homing workers plodded across the park, observing with curiosity the fire-engines in the distance, when Rudi Bittesch was sitting in his flat at St John's Wood trying, without success, to telephone to Jane at the club to speak to her privately, the Labour government was new-born, and elsewhere on the face of the globe people slept, queued for liberations, beat the tom-toms, took shelter from the bombers, or went for a ride on the dodgem at the fun-fair. (*GSM*, p. 127)

76

Such a world will not, Spark's novel implies, be saved by a series of selfish gestures.

*

In 1963, the year in which *The Girls of Slender Means* appeared, Muriel Spark was quoted in an interview as saying she was 'writing minor novels deliberately, and not major novels', and that she eschewed the ambition of being 'Mrs Tolstoy, you know'.[52] At the same time, paradoxically, she was planning her largest novel, *The Mandelbaum Gate* (1965), having spent two months of 1961 in Israel amassing material for an exploration of her ethnic origins. Originally, *The Mandelbaum Gate* was conceived as an experimental exercise in autobiography, examining the lives of three generations of women represented by the author, her mother and her grandmother.[53] A short story, 'The Gentile Jewesses' (published in 1963 in *Winter's Tales No. 9*) probably originated as an attempt to cast the novel in first-personal form. It begins by recalling Spark's grandmother's general shop in Watford, alludes to her father's position as an engineer, and notes:

> I was a Gentile Jewess like my grandmother, for my father was a Jew. . . . I thought of [my mother] as the second Gentile Jewess after my grandmother, and myself as the third. . . . To [my parents] it was no great shock when I turned Catholic, since with Roman Catholics too, it all boils down to the Almighty in the end. (*Bang-Bang You're Dead and Other Stories*, pp. 46–9)

The Mandelbaum Gate follows the quest for her own identity of the heroine, Barbara Vaughan, which she can only resolve by reconciling the extremes of her personality and feeling 'all of a piece, a Gentile Jewess, a private-judging Catholic, a shy adventuress' (*MG*, p. 164). Before Barbara's duality dissolves into these oxymorons she has to cross the distance between physical appearance and psychological reality. Several of the characters she encounters in the Holy Land behave in ways that contradict the qualities they project to the world. Freddy Hamilton, the quiet diplomat, acts impulsively at a climactic juncture; Miss Rickward, the spinster headmistress of the English school where Barbara teaches, goes to bed with the double-dealing Jordanian travel-agent Joe Ramdez; a conventional colleague of Freddy's turns out to be a spy. Barbara, externally composed, finds romantic resources in herself.

It is the existential contention of Miss Rickward – who can 'discourse for hours on the history and development of the existentialist philosophy' (p. 154) – that existence precedes essence, a doctrine that ripples over the surface of *The Mandelbaum Gate*. According to existentialist theory, each individual apprehends existence in terms of subjective experience and the immediate situation; the problem of existence is understood in terms of the impact which experiences have on a particular existent. The principal characters in *The Mandelbaum Gate* suppose that they are part of an ordered universe and so subject to natural laws which govern human behaviour. Their assumptions are tested by the events Spark incorporates in her novel.

Spark does not often allow her characters to acquire an existence beyond the constraints of a plot and she has come to dislike *The Mandelbaum Gate*: 'I don't like that book awfully much. . . . In the beginning it's slow, and the end is very rapid, it races. . . . I got bored, because it was too long, so I decided never again to write a long book, keep them very short.'[54] Actually *The Mandelbaum Gate* is one of Spark's most profound performances and her criticism of it is doubtless motivated by more than technical misgivings. It is probable that she regretted the tone of the book, because she, like her partly autobiographical heroine Barbara Vaughan, became too emotionally involved in the plot. She has said, after all, 'I think it's bad manners to inflict a lot of emotional involvement on the reader – much nicer to make them laugh and keep it short.'[55] Spark likes to keep a tight control on her characters and keep them to the confines of her story. *The Mandelbaum Gate* differs from most Spark novels in that the characters engage the reader's empathy, thus escaping from the fictional structure.

The main action of *The Mandelbaum Gate* occurs in 1961; though the usual Sparkian flashbacks and flashforwards make the fictional time fluid, the year is a decisive factor in the novel. Israel has launched its first guided rocket and the country is traumatically shocked by the trial of the Nazi mass-murderer Adolf

Eichmann. Like Spark in 1961, Barbara Vaughan visits the Eichmann trial and there sees a man catastrophically caught in his past. Eichmann is presented, as Allan Massie has noted, as 'a ghastly parody of the believer'.[56] He does not, to recall the existential overtones of the novel, understand his own existence in terms of subjective experience:

> [Eichmann] went on repeating his lines which were punctuated by the refrain, *Bureau IV-B-4*. Barbara felt she was caught in a conspiracy to prevent her brain from functioning. . . . The man was plainly not testifying for himself, but for his pre-written destiny. He was not answering for himself or his own life at all, but for an imperative deity named Bureau IV-B-4, of whom he was the High Priest. . . . [Eichmann] patiently expounded, once more, the complex theology in which not his own actions, nor even Hitler's, were the theme of his defence, but the honour of the Supreme Being, the system, and its least tributary, Bureau IV-B-4. (*MG*, p. 179)

Though the Eichmann trial, 'a highly religious trial' (p. 180), is introduced obliquely into the book, its impact on Barbara is immense. Through it she confronts the consequences of a false faith. It is after her visit to the trial that she decides to complete her pilgrimage to the Holy Land in Jordan – where she risks danger as a Jew.

In 1961, the year of Barbara's visit to the Holy Land, the Mandelbaum Gate divides Jerusalem: symbolically it splits Jerusalem from itself. It is thus a suitable place for Barbara to be as she is, temperamentally and geographically, in 'a state of conflict' (p. 23). As a 'half-Jew' (p. 27) she feels able to express her sexuality with Harry Clegg, her lover; as a Catholic convert she is theologically certain (at least at the beginning of the novel) that she should not marry Harry, a divorced man, unless his first marriage is invalidated by the Church. 'Searching her own motives like a murder squad' (p. 46), Barbara finds herself in a Holy Land itself divided by the conflicting claims of mutually hostile religions. Israel, which attracts the Jewish part of her, is clearly in a combative state of conflict. Its assertive existence, its triumph over adversity, encourages her to dwell on her own duality: on the one hand a Jew, on the other a Catholic convert; on the one hand a settled spinster of 37 with a safe job back home teaching English in a Gloucestershire girls' school, on the other a passionate pilgrim sexually involved with Harry Clegg. Harry, following his archaeological profession at the Dead Sea excavations while Barbara is in the Holy Land, satisfies Barbara's physical appetite only. She hears an English priest observe, while provocatively saying Mass at the Church of the Holy Sepulchre, 'If you are looking for physical exactitude in Jerusalem it is a good quest, but it belongs to archaeology, not faith' (p. 198). Barbara wants both the facts and the faith.

Barbara's sense of uncertainty is rooted in her past, a burden she carries with her to the Holy Land. Fictional flashbacks establish that she spent half the vacations of her youth with her Jewish mother in Golders Green, the other half with her father's fox-hunting folk at Bells Sands, Worcestershire. In the Holy Land she wonders 'Who am I?' (p. 28) and feels she owes an explanation to the Polish Israeli guide to whom she has identified herself as 'A half-Jew. . . . Through my mother' (p. 27) and a Catholic convert. The physical location encourages metaphysical considerations of the meaning of duality:

> They entered Caesarea, home of ancient disputations, while she attempted to acquaint the guide with the Golders Green Jewishness of her mother's relations and the rural Anglicanism of her father's, the Passover gatherings on the one hand and the bell-summoned Evensongs on the other, the talkative intellectuals of the one part and the kennel-keeping blood sportsmen of the other. . . . [The guide] was demanding a definition. By the long habit of her life, and by temperament, she held as a vital principle that the human mind was bound in duty to continuous acts of definition. Mystery was acceptable to her, but only under the aspect of a crown of thorns. (pp. 28–9)

Barbara's faith has yet to accommodate her as an indivisible individual.

In her search for the essence of her own identity, Barbara remembers how she stayed with her cousin in St Albans the summer before the pilgrimage to the Holy Land. Though her evenings were supposedly spent baby-sitting and discussing archaeology with Harry Clegg, in fact 'Barbara and Harry Clegg were in the spare bedroom, making love' (p. 40). Barbara's search for an identity beyond the illusion of appearance is the substance of *The Mandelbaum Gate*. In a world where people act according to the labels pinned on them (teacher, diplomat, archaeologist) she seeks the truth about herself, sure that she is more than 'a spinster of no fixed identity' (p. 47). That she concentrates her quest on the Holy Land is crucial to the theme, for there the gap between appearance and reality is complicated by religious ritual and political intrigue. Barbara, Spark shows, is as complex as any social phenomenon. To the Foreign Office diplomat Freddy Hamilton, Barbara seems on first impression 'a pleasant English spinster' (p. 16). The label is discarded as Freddy discovers that Barbara can be far from conventionally English and pleasant. First, he learns that she is both Jewish and Catholic. Second, he hears of her involvement with Harry Clegg. Third, she rudely rebukes Freddy's frivolity by quoting to him a passage from the Book of the Apocalypse:

> I know of thy doings, and find thee neither cold nor hot; cold or hot. I would thou wert one or the other. Being what thou art, lukewarm, neither cold nor hot, thou wilt make me vomit thee out of my mouth. (p. 21)

Freddy has been warned and in the interests of Barbara's search for herself must act out of character. Barbara's discovery of herself is assisted by a change in Freddy's behaviour.

Early in the novel Freddy is presented as a human cipher; his code is careerism and he is a comparatively free agent with diplomatic immunity to pass through the Mandelbaum Gate, from Israel to Jordan, every weekend. His only interesting trait seems to be his penchant for composing formal verses of thanks to Joanna Cartwright, his hostess in Jordan. A subplot, which unfolds in fragments through the novel, puts Freddy in a more complicated context and suggests he is more than the sum of his professional parts. Now 55, he has once been married to 'a bad lot' (p. 146) and has a family secret. Back in Harrogate his septuagenarian mother lives the life of a 'tyrant-liar' (p. 60) whose faults are ignored by the family but irksome to the old servant Miss Bennett – 'Benny', a religious maniac. Troubled by Barbara Vaughan's presence in Jordan where she could conceivably be arrested as an Israeli spy – 'Anyone with Jewish blood is automatically arrested as an Israeli spy', Freddy tells Barbara (p. 78) – he decides to act according to passion rather than to rely on reason. Receiving the usual letters of complaint from his mother (accusing Benny of stealing) and from Benny (accusing his mother of being in league with the Devil) he first replies to them, then decides to rid himself of their lingering influence on him. Going to the Jordanian shop of Alexandros – an Arab dealer and Orthodox-Catholic from the Lebanon – he takes the letters and his replies, burns them and flushes them down the toilet. It is a satisfyingly symbolic act, purging himself of an old problem and leaving him free to deal with the predicament of Barbara Vaughan.

Barbara's journey from Israel to Jordan raises the whole question of her identity. She obtains an extra passport and a baptismal certificate, documents that certify her as being an English spinster and a Catholic. Thus confirmed in her 'old identity' (*MG*, p. 188) Barbara goes to St Helena's Convent as though in retreat from the reality of her pilgrimage. Before leaving Israel, she had hoped to hear from Harry Clegg but had instead received two unexpected letters from England. One, from 'Ricky' – Miss Rickward – accuses her of having an affair with Harry (a fact of Spark's fiction); the other, from her cousin Michael Aaronson, announces his intention of attending the Eichmann trial in his legal capacity. Barbara acts on the basis of the epistles from England: she explains to Ricky that she no longer wishes to work at the girls' school, and it is Michael's arrival in Israel that gives her her glimpse of the appalling Eichmann, the fanatical adherent to a false faith. With Harry in Rome, seeking an annulment of his previous marriage, Barbara feels alone with the actuality of her existence, since she has abandoned her job (with Ricky), her illusions (on seeing Eichmann) and her religious objections to the marriage with Harry – telling him, 'I'm going to marry you anyway' (p. 181).

In Jordan, Barbara is concealed in a convent, isolated from others. Dramatically, Freddy Hamilton comes to her rescue. Having burned the correspondence with his mother and Benny, he feels free for the first time in his life. Aided and abetted by Alexandros, the Arab dealer, Freddy extricates Barbara from the convent, assuring her that she is in peril as a Jewish woman in Jordan. He takes her from the convent to the Potter's Field, where she is safely received by an old Greek Orthodox monk. Barbara is left to reflect on the import of her actions:

> Now Barbara lay awake, marvelling at her escape from the convent. . . . She thought, it's like the enactment of a reluctant nun's dream, and she laughed softly in the darkness, thinking of the absurdity of the phrase 'escape from the convent' that had kept recurring in their conversation in the car, on the way to the Potter's Field. . . . But it had been an escape of a kind, as witness to which she could cite her present sense of release. . . . The reality of the hour was her escape from the convent. . . . She thought, it was really very funny, that escape from the convent. . . . It was not any escape from any real convent, it was an unidentified confinement of the soul she had escaped from. (pp. 163–5)

Spark could not make the symbolism any clearer: by reiterating the phrase 'escape from the convent' she stresses that Barbara has cast off the cloak of her old identity. She is no longer nun-like, no longer wrapping her religion protectively around her, no longer a Jew in Israel, no longer conforming to the expectations of her appearance, no longer safe. She is, like Freddy in his defiance of the epistles from Harrogate, cut off from her immediate past. In existential terms she has, for the moment, abandoned her *mauvaise foi* and is free to shape her own destiny through a succession of choices for which she is totally responsible.

In a Sartrian novel, Barbara would henceforth bear the burden of her responsibility; the Sparkian novel, however, cannot ignore the impact of the environment. Barbara's new-found freedom is as much of an illusion as her old identity; she has to disguise herself in order to exist in Jordan. As she knows the Jordanian police are looking for her, she dons a veil and dresses as an old Arab woman. Barbara continues her pilgrimage by pretending to be the servant of Joe Ramdez's daughter Suzi, a promiscuous girl of 33 who sleeps regularly with Alexandros and subsequently with Freddy

Hamilton. When Barbara, in her disguise, visits the Holy Sepulchre, she sees Ricky, who has followed her to the Holy Land intent on destroying her relationship with Harry Clegg. Though Barbara and Ricky come face to face – Ricky being 'within breathing distance of Barbara's veil' (*MG*, p. 203) – the disguise protects Barbara. After this encounter, Barbara succumbs to scarlet fever. An infectious disease has been traced to St Helena's Convent, where Barbara stayed, but the symbolic tone of the narrative suggests that her illness is psychosomatic. Lying in bed, discussing sexual allure in a house also inhabited by Joe Ramdez's 'pretty prostitutes' (p. 233), Barbara tells Suzi Ramdez, 'I'm the scarlet woman' (p. 232). The pun points up the distance between appearance and actuality. Barbara is neither a nun nor a scarlet woman.

Well aware that her father is a political informer for the Jordanian Secret Service and that he keeps prostitutes in his house at Jericho, Suzi nevertheless thinks Barbara will be safe there. The house itself has Christian connotations; it is an old Crusader church in the foundation, therefore 'the spirit of the Crusaders in their everyday aspect brooded over the house' (p. 246). In this house occur a number of incidents that advance the already involved plot. Freddy realizes it is 'Nasser's Post Office' (p. 224) when he sees Ruth Gardnor, wife of one of his diplomatic colleagues, plant a note in a tree; Freddy is seduced by Suzi into believing that 'love is life' (p. 222); Ruth Gardnor convinces herself (mistaking appearance for actuality) that Barbara is a spy in the same organization as herself. As for Barbara, she physically attacks Ruth after despairing of her violent anti-Semitism and finds Ricky sharing the bed of Joe Ramdez, an event that precedes Ricky's marriage to Ramdez and 'her eager embrace of Islam' (p. 242).

Realizing that she has substituted one disguise for another, Barbara returns to Israel with Abdul Ramdez, Suzi's brother, and looks forward to marriage with Harry Clegg, a marriage blessed by another Sparkian irony. Ricky has falsified Harry's birth certificate, making him a baptized Roman Catholic, in the hope that this will prevent the annulment of his previous marriage. Actually it nullifies that marriage and the reader is told, in a parody of the happy ending, that 'Barbara and Harry were married and got along fairly well together ever after' (p. 303). Barbara's pilgrimage has given her an insight into herself as a woman with both physical needs and metaphysical longings. She is, finally, able to face facts as well as to acknowledge that the ideals of her faith are flexible.

Freddy Hamilton's part in Barbara's pilgrimage leaves him with amnesia complicated by the news that Benny has murdered his mother in Harrogate. Spark suggests that Freddy 'obliterated these days from his memory' (p. 167), though Barbara Vaughan knows better than the narrator:

> It was unforgettable. The whole week was unforgettable, and Suzi most of all. [Barbara] wondered, later, how it was that Freddy had forgotten Suzi Ramdez. And, of course, the question answered itself: she had been too memorable to remember. (p. 280)

Freddy's sexual passion with Suzi is renounced for practical purposes, only flooding back briefly in a glowing memory. Barbara, however, understands that some aspects of reality have to be rejected:

> She was thinking of the Eichmann trial, and was aware that there were other events too, which had rolled away the stone that revealed an empty hole in the earth, that led to a bottomless pit. So that people drew back quickly and looked elsewhere for reality, and found it, and made decisions, in the way that she had decided to get married, anyway. (p. 282)

The existential solution is intolerable, Spark insinuates; facts need to be filtered through fictions.

The Mandelbaum Gate deals in detail with subjects that are subsumed in Spark's more selective novels. She shows, for example, an ability to make creative comments on political issues. Abdul Ramdez, who teaches Freddy Hamilton Arabic and assists Barbara in her escape from Jordan, is an intelligent Arab bored by 'the mentality that now presented to every Arab in Palestine the blood-duty of becoming a professional victim' (p. 100). As a Palestinian Arab, Abdul consorts with his Jewish friends in Acre

85

where he can keep the company of those he likes regardless of political colour or ethnic creed. One passage in particular sums up Spark's ironic attitude to the politics of the Middle East:

> Just before he had left hospital, Abdul had got a brief note in Suzi's handwriting. 'How are Abdul's orange groves thriving?' He puzzled for a few moments, then smiled. The displaced poor were already being urged to recall the extent of the lands and possessions from which they had fled before the Israelis' onslaught. More and more, the bewildered homeless souls, in thousands and tens of thousands, agreed and then convinced themselves, and were to hold for long years to come, that they had, every man of them, been driven from vast holdings in their bit of Palestine, from green hilly pastures and so many acres of lush orange groves as would have covered Arabia. (p. 100)

It is another illusion, another example of self-deception; another illustration of the human tendency to live by lies, by arbitrary creeds, by patriotic credos. Against this background, Barbara's quest amounts to a series of escapes. *The Mandelbaum Gate*, in describing these escapes, is not an escapist work in the literary meaning of that term. It does, however, recognize the need to escape from the tyranny of dogma, to live without splitting the self into absolute good and total evil.

4

TOWARDS THE ONLY PROBLEM

Since 1968 Muriel Spark has veered between compact variants on earlier themes, outrageously satirical scenarios and experimental alternatives to the kind of book she produced in *The Mandelbaum Gate*. Thus *Loitering with Intent* (1981) is clearly kin to *The Comforters* in the material it assesses, while *The Only Problem* (1984) is a variation on a theme inherent in that first novel. Spark broadens the scope of her satire in several books, bringing Italian sensationalism into *The Public Image* (1968), the Watergate scandal into *The Abbess of Crewe* (1974), the crisis of capitalism into *The Takeover* (1976) and political terrorism into *Territorial Rights* (1979). In *The Driver's Seat* (1970), *Not to Disturb* (1971) and *The Hothouse by the East River* (1973) her avoidance of inward psychological depiction invites a comparison between this aspect of her output and the work of the *nouveaux romanciers*. During this development of her writing Spark has continued to consider the nature of fiction and the resilience of characters who struggle against fictions of their own or the author's creation. Many of these books call into question the major relations of fiction: between external author and internal characters, between creative artists and destructive agents, between plots that are artistically contrived and plots that are concocted by criminal plotters. The artistry is as self-conscious as ever, the manipulation of fictional ploys assured.

In 1966 Muriel Spark settled in Rome (where she still lives) and two years later she published her first Roman novel. Finding the sustained effort of two years' work on *The Mandelbaum Gate* artistically unrewarding (though many readers find rich rewards of their own) she returned to the concise format of her earlier fiction. *The Public Image* may present an unusual figure in Spark's canon – a film-star of limited intelligence, utterly unlike the intellectual women Caroline Rose (*The Comforters*), January Marlow (*Robinson*) and Barbara Vaughan (*The Mandelbaum Gate*) – but the theme and techniques of the book utilize familiar features from Spark's established style. Inevitably, the distance between appearance and actuality is invoked, as is the interdependence of fact and fiction. Stylistically, the novel is narrated by a detached observer who never becomes emotionally involved in the story. It has been suggested that Spark identifies with the heroine of *The Public Image* because, by the time she came to Rome, she was critically and commercially successful on a grand scale, 'her apartment, her jewellery and her couture clothes reflecting the commercial standing of her work and contributing to her glossy image'.[57] Yet it would be misleading to read *The Public Image* as in any sense an autobiographically inclined novel. Having exhaustively investigated her own nature in *The Mandelbaum Gate* Spark must have turned with relief to the task of writing *The Public Image*. It presents select scenes from the life of a woman professionally divorced from reality.

Annabel Christopher is 'a puny little thing . . . a little chit of a thing . . . a little slip of a thing' (*PI*, pp. 7–8) who is transformed into an object of desire in 'Italy, the Motherland of Sensation' (p. 24). Born in Wakefield, she goes to drama school, meets and marries another aspiring actor, Frederick Christopher, and lives with him in London (Kensington, of course). Typecast as a dull, colourless creature in English films, she is artistically enlarged in Rome by Luigi Leopardi, an Italian producer, who perceives that Annabel's lustrous eyes are her greatest cinematic asset. Remaking her in the public image of the 'English Tiger-Lady' (p. 22), Luigi unleashes his press secretary Francesca on a publicity campaign for Annabel's first starring role. Accordingly, Francesca makes a cult of the English couple:

[Francesca] made Frederick and Annabel into a famous couple, impeccably formal by the light of day, voluptuously enamoured with each other under cover of night. . . . *Minerva Arrives at Platform 10* was made, released, and applauded. Sexy Annabel was now photographed for nice English magazines and was shown on television, at the races, wearing a country coat and a meek brimmed hat. . . . Annabel was now part of a world of Oscars and film festival prizes; although she was not yet cited for any of these awards, still she was assumed to be in the running for them. (pp. 23, 28, 29)

Spark's prose here is coolly informative, journalistic in its bland presentation of the contours of Annabel's career.

Spark's fascination with the relationship between personality and role-playing is central to *The Public Image*; in the novel she shows a woman becoming the character others have invented for her. The shy, vulnerable English girl-next-door becomes, off as well as on screen, the English Tiger-Lady. She conforms to the fiction of her public image. Spark supplies Annabel with a crisis she can build into a climax, thanks to her experience as an actress. For while Annabel goes from cinematic strength to strength, Frederick feels himself an adjunct to her glamorous reputation. After sleeping apart for months, thus failing to live up to Annabel's public image, they come together, 'by mutual agreement' (p. 30), so that Annabel can have a baby. That, at least, is how Frederick interprets events. 'And the baby,' he tells her, 'the baby's only in aid of your public image' (p. 30). Annabel defends herself and her image: 'What's wrong with my public image? It's a good one. I'm a faithful wife, not a tart' (p. 30). Once Annabel was content to act according to the scripts Frederick wrote for her; in Rome, however, she is the creation of Luigi Leopardi and his publicity machine. Frederick cannot tolerate the change in Annabel; he wants a subservient wife, not a celebrity.

To further her career, Annabel settles with Frederick in Rome, the perfect setting for the events that unfold. In the Italian press, Spark says, 'The range of emotions was as grand as Grand Opera, but no subtler' (p. 23), while Rome is ruled by 'the Seven Capital Sins . . . pride, covetousness, lust, anger, gluttony, envy and sloth' (p. 24). Emotional excess and sensation are everywhere in Rome, a situation that suits Annabel's public image. After the couple have moved into a hotel in Rome, the increasingly independent Annabel finds a flat on the first floor of a sixteenth-century *palazzo* containing a cross-section of Roman society. The ideal English couple are, in actuality, incompatible. Frederick achieves some happiness with an Italian girlfriend, Marina, while Annabel anticipates an affair with Luigi Leopardi. Annabel's public image is a fiction; her baby, Carl, is 'the only reality of her life' (p. 35).

A skilful scriptwriter, Frederick contrives a scenario that, he hopes, will ruin Annabel. First, he tells his friends to descend on Annabel's flat for a party she knows nothing about; second, he takes his own life by jumping from the planks covering the caves under the Church of St John and St Paul, landing in 'the foundations where they have placed the martyrdom of St Paul' (p. 56). For his finale he has left suicide notes suggesting that he was driven to despair over Annabel's addiction to orgies. He dies feeling he has ruined her public image, confident that the Italian press will concoct a scandal from the clues he has scattered. He has not reckoned with Annabel's ability to adopt her fictional persona as a fact.

Annabel obtains the suicide notes from Billy O'Brien, Frederick's friend, then uses her acquired acting expertise to persuade the press that she is a widow devastated by the loss of a beloved husband. It is a part she plays to perfection. She rises to the occasion, determined to ensure 'the survival of a public image under threat' (p. 70). Before the inquest on Frederick's death she discovers that Billy O'Brien has photocopies of the suicide notes and is intent on blackmailing her for money. Nonplussed, she acknowledges the existence of the notes at the inquest, explaining 'there is no truth in what my husband accuses me of in those letters. He was insane' (p. 123). She then goes to the airport, with her baby, to take a plane to Greece. She wants to get away from Rome 'to be free like my baby' (p. 123). The reader is left to guess whether she can ever discard her public image.

Superficially, the plot of the novel reads like one of Annabel's films: the jealous husband, the falsely accused wife, the melodramatic death in the catacombs, the final triumph over adversity. Annabel is fated, it seems, to perform roles written for her. By recording Annabel's progress from fictional reality to cinematic fantasy as a typically Roman routine, Spark takes a creative risk

90

and the novel is, as a result, her most prosaic work. However, *The Public Image* is given the benefit of one poetic touch, a final sentence that gives metaphorical force to an image outlined earlier in the book. In his suicide note to Annabel, Frederick describes his wife as 'a beautiful shell, like something washed up on the sea-shore, a collector's item, perfectly formed, a pearly shell – but empty, devoid of the life it once held' (p. 92). At the airport, travelling incognito, Annabel is unrecognized, bereft of her public image:

> She was as pale as a shell. . . . Nobody recognized her as she stood, having moved the baby to rest on her hip, conscious also of the baby in a sense weightlessly and perpetually within her, as an empty shell contains, by its very structure, the echo and harking image of former and former seas. (pp. 124–5)

The final image is a private one; Annabel's emptiness is an ache to create something more enduring than herself.

*

Spark's wholly poetic approach returns with a vengeance (witness the sinister subject-matter) in her next three novels, which can be read as a thematically interwoven trio. Since *The Comforters* Spark's interest in free will has been evident, for she continually considers the challenge of choice in a world dominated by deterministic theory and materialistic philosophy. As a Catholic she believes that beyond grim reality soars a spiritual idea; as a novelist she is aware that literary conventions generally determine the actions of various characters. Fiction is, traditionally, a deterministic form, yet Spark wishes to persuade the reader that life should not be taken for granted, as a *fait accompli*, as a matter of going through the motions. To illuminate this insight she chooses to combine three fictional modes in a poetic manner: the neo-Gothic adventure, the surrealistic fantasy and the *nouveau roman*.

Spark's book on Mary Shelley, *Child of Light* (1951), discusses the connections between the Gothic novel and surrealism. Shelley's *Frankenstein* (1818) is, for Spark, 'the first of a new and hybrid fictional species . . . both the apex and the last of Gothic fiction'.[58] *Frankenstein*, Spark argues, is not a 'terror' novel but a 'horror' novel since it conveys 'disgust as well as dismay', not 'merely panic and alarm'.[59] The neo-Gothic technique of *Frankenstein* impresses Spark as an adumbration of surrealism, a movement anxious to simulate the disjointed quality of the dream. To the neo-Gothic and surrealistic modes she adds the experimental impasse of the *nouveau roman*. Alain Robbe-Grillet's *Les Gommes* (1953) and *Le Voyeur* (1955) show characters cut off from a physical reality beyond their control; in the discursive *Pour un Nouveau Roman* (1963) Robbe-Grillet dwells on the distance between individuals and the physical objects that surround them. To the anti-novelist the individual, then, is alone in an indifferent world of objects. Spark's attitude to the anti-novel is indicated in *The Mandelbaum Gate*, when Barbara Vaughan recoils from the cold calculations of Eichmann, the mass-murderer who computes a massacre in numerical terms:

> She thought, it all feels like a familiar dream, and presently located the sensation as one that the anti-novelists induce. . . . At school she usually took the novels and plays of the new French writers with the sixth form. She thought, repetition, boredom, despair, going nowhere for nothing, all of which conditions are enclosed in a tight, unbreakable statement of the times at hand. (*MG*, p. 177)

It interests Spark as an experimental option but it is not enough: by adding neo-Gothic and surrealistic touches to the anti-novel, however, she evolved a chilling format to suit her own purposes.

Spark excels at evoking the enigmatic overtones of modern life. In her three thematically related novels – *The Driver's Seat* (1970), *Not to Disturb* (1971), *The Hothouse on the East River* (1973) – she makes a prolonged raid on the bizarre. All three novels are written in the present tense and Spark must have kept both senses of the word 'tense' in her mind, for the books are as full of tension as they are of immediacy. They suggest the coexistence of fact and fantasy, exhibit a surrealistic ambiguity, and allow dreams to dissolve into nightmares. In the traditional novel the author knows all; in the first of Spark's quintessentially poetic trio of novels the author is not so sure of her heroine, for 'Who knows her thoughts? Who can tell?' (*DS*, p. 50).

92

The Driver's Seat is the study of a willing sacrificial victim. Lise, a 34-year-old office worker, flies south to organize her own murder. In order to attract the maximum attention she dresses in an outrageous outfit – red and white striped coat; purple, orange and blue skirt; yellow top – which provokes the hilarity of onlookers who, when the events of the novel are over, will become witnesses with good cause to remember this particular victim. Lise is conspicuous by her colourful presence. She is obsessively in search of a man who is, to use her favourite expression, her type. To drive home the macabre nature of the situation Spark elevates prolepsis to a stylistic principle. Chapter 3 begins by giving the game away, so depriving the reader of a major element of surprise:

> She will be found tomorrow morning dead from multiple stab-wounds, her wrists bound with a silk scarf and her ankles bound with a man's necktie in the grounds of an empty villa, in a park of the foreign city to which she is travelling on the flight now boarding at Gate 14. (*DS*, p. 25)

Lise chooses for her murderer a rosy-faced young businessman who conforms to her type. For much of the book he is conspicuous by his absence; then he reappears for the bloody climax the book has been inexorably reaching for. At first the man avoids Lise's attentions; when she sits near him on the plane he moves away. Lise talks instead to Bill, a food faddist about to set up a macrobiotic establishment in Naples. Explaining to Lise that his macrobiotic regime demands an orgasm a day, he wonders if she will oblige him that evening. As he takes her to her hotel in a taxi he makes a pass at her and spills his macrobiotic seed on the floor. This sexual metaphor is at once comic and revealing. Lise, it seems, is not interested in sustaining life through sex.

All the symbols are substantiated in this way. Lise assumes the driver's seat, literally and figuratively, to proclaim that in a deterministic universe she will nevertheless choose her own destiny. Eventually her dream seems about to come true when she finds her perfect homicidal type – the man from the plane. Lise presents him with a knife, although she knows, intuitively, that he is a sex maniac recently charged with attempted murder. She persuades him to come with her in the car and, once more in the driver's seat, she takes him to a park. She instructs him exactly how to kill her and he carries out every instruction but one. Readers aware of Spark's meticulous attention to language will realize that her pun on 'plunges' makes it plain that the murderer ignores Lise's request to desist from sexual penetration:

> 'I don't want any sex,' she shouts. 'You can have it after-wards. Tie my feet and kill, that's all. They will come and sweep it up in the morning.'
> All the same, he plunges into her, with the knife poised high.
> 'Kill me,' she says, and repeats it in four languages. (*DS*, p. 106)

This shock ending is ironical in the extreme. Lise's dream of manipulating the precise manner of her death is destroyed by her murderer's refusal to accept her every instruction. By choosing, by exercising his free will against her authority, he diminishes her dream, transforms it into a nightmare.

The deaths in *Not to Disturb*, the second book in the macabre poetic trilogy, are preordained according to a commercial plan, so there is no element of suspense, simply an exposition and its inevitable resolution. Three characters are certain to die violently in the novel, namely the Baron and Baroness Klopstock and Victor Passerat, the Baroness's lover: 'They die of violence,' says Clovis, who studies contractual documents; 'To be precise, it is of violence that they shortly die' (*ND*, p. 13). 'They haunt the house,' says Lister the Baron's butler, 'like insubstantial bodies, while still alive' (p. 23). Spark uses the Baron's doomed house, near Geneva, as an arena for the exercise of her ironic wit and surrealistic sense of humour. At an important point in the narrative it transpires that Heloise, a maid, is probably pregnant by the Baron's younger brother, an idiot kept in the attic. A Reverend is summoned to marry the couple, thus ensuring that the Klopstock family fortune will remain in the control of the servants. The entry of the imbecile is a superb parody of the Gothic mode:

> The zestful cretin's eyes fall first on Irene [another maid]. He neighs jubilantly through his large teeth and shakes his long white wavy hair. He wears a jump-suit of dark red velvet

94

fastened from crotch to collar-bone with a zip-fastener. This zipper is secured at the neck by a tiny padlock which very likely has been taken, for the purpose, from one of the Baroness Klopstock's Hermes handbags. . . . At the moment he seems to prefer Irene, and, breaking loose, plunges upon her. . . . But now the captive has caught sight of the bride [Heloise], tall, pink and plump, and indicates his welcome with a huge fanfare of delight, straining mightily towards her. (pp. 74–5)

Like the imbecile, the 'insubstantial bodies' of the Klopstocks and Victor Passerat are incidental to the plot. The focal point of the book is Lister, a servant whose ingenuity makes Figaro look naive.

Not To Disturb portrays people who exist without recognizably human emotions. Like *The Driver's Seat*, it relies on prolepsis. Lister stage-manages the aftermath of a violent event (before that event has happened) – the suicide of the Baron after he has murdered the Baroness and her lover Victor Passerat. Lister has arranged a press conference, sold the movie rights of the sensational story, and has a cinematographer and sound-track man on hand. Mr Samuel, the cinematographer, thinks the whole plot a 'first-rate movie script' (*ND*, p. 58) as there is a Gothic mood of menace, a symbolic storm and a cast of eccentrics including the imbecile brother in the attic. Spark is, again, making a verbal assault on the idea of a deterministic universe; in her life and her art she insists on free will. Lister, for example, explains that his own plot is a foregone conclusion: 'To all intents and purposes, they're already dead although as a matter of banal fact, the night's business has still to accomplish itself' (p. 12).

As a matter of equally banal fact, a novel is normally narrated in a deterministic manner. Spark's poetic approach queries the role of the novelist as surrogate God and solipsistic creator. By playing conceptual games with the reader Spark suggests that life, like art, should never be treated as a foregone conclusion. The title of her novel is appropriately ironic. The Baron has given orders that the servants are not to disturb him. Yet they are more than disturbing – they are all-devouring. They package him and market him while he is still alive, thus turning a character into a commodity. Spark compresses her novel into an overwhelming image of an infernal world populated by citizens whose speciality is the denial of life. A world devoid of free will would be as soul-destroying as Lister's scenario.

'One should live first, then die, not die then live; everything to its own time' (*HER*, p. 119). That sentence poignantly informs the fantasy *The Hothouse by the East River*, which is told, like the other two powerfully poetic novels, in the present tense. It concerns a group of ghosts who have been brought into collective consciousness by the restlessness of one of them – Paul Hazlett, a reluctant corpse whose 'heart knocks on the sides of the coffin' (p. 127). Paul lives in a posh New York apartment with his wife Elsa, whose shadow falls in the wrong direction. Spark introduces a suspenseful element into the novel by bringing Elsa into contact with Helmut Kiel, a double agent she last glimpsed in 1944. Paul would be alarmed were it not that he can rationalize on the impossibility of it all, for he knows that he and Elsa were killed in 1944, at St Pancras station, when a V-2 bomb fell directly on the train in which they were sitting. The novel thus explores the life Paul and Elsa might have had if they had settled in New York after the war, if they had had two children, if they had acquired enough money to live in comfort. They have a life, nevertheless, as literary creations that hover between the reality the reader invests them with and the illusion the author attributes to them. Spark is alive to the way so many people – in life and in art – accept a death-in-life. When Paul and Elsa watch the ghosts of friends who died with them in 1944, she says, 'You would think they were alive,' and he adds, 'One can't tell the difference' (p. 135).

Even as she teases the reader with fantasies and tricks them with poetic ploys that disrupt the narrative, Spark has a serious purpose. Her novels do not evade what governments recognize as reality, as witness her catalogue in *The Hothouse by the East River*:

> We already have the youth problem, the racist problem, the distribution problem, the political problem, the economic problem, the crime problem, the matrimonial problem, the ecological problem, the divorce problem, the domiciliary problem, the consumer problem, the birth-rate problem, the middle-age problem, the health problem, the sex problem, the incarceration problem, the educational problem, the fiscal problem, the

unemployment problem, the physiopsychodynamics problem, the homosexual problem, the traffic problem, the obesity problem, the heterosexual problem. . . . (p. 108)

Spark's overall poetic tone implies that this level of reality is itself an illusion and that those who are aware of it alone are as good as dead since they refuse to relate to a more intense form of existence.

The Hothouse by the East River is a ghost story with darkly comic incidents and suitably surrealistic overtones. The use of humour is often outrageous. For example, Elsa's bosom friend Princess Xavier has a farm of sheep and silkworms. She habitually keeps the eggs of her silkworms warm by, literally, taking them to her bosom. Garven Bey, the analyst, witnesses the result of a grotesque gestation:

> Garven screams. His eyes are on the Princess's bosom. He screams. Under the protective folds of her breasts the Princess, this very morning, has concealed for warmth and fear of the frost a precious new consignment of mulberry leaves bearing numerous eggs of silk-worms. These have hatched in the heat. The worms themselves now celebrate life by wriggling upon Princess Xavier's breast and causing Garven to scream. (p. 45)

Shortly after this, Garven abandons his professional calling and becomes Elsa's manservant.

Elsa's eccentricity is acceptable in New York, where (Spark implies) contemporary urban life is as bizarre as any work of fiction. Elsa does exactly as the mood takes her. When she wants to see if her shoe salesman is Kiel she goes to Zurich to have an affair with him and tells Paul, in a long-distance phone-call, 'I slept with him last night. I don't think he's Kiel' (p. 71). Appearance and reality, art and artifice, dissolve into each other in this book. Elsa returns to New York for her son Pierre's production of Barrie's *Peter Pan*. The novelty is in the casting, as all the parts will be taken by sexagenarians to prove Pierre's contention that '*Peter Pan* is a very obscene play' (p. 63). Elsa causes a sensation at the première of Pierre's production by throwing tomatoes at the cast: chaos follows but Elsa takes it in her stride. It seems apt in Spark's New York that there is so little substantial difference between ghosts and the solid citizens.

Elsa and Paul are, though apparently authentic, ghosts twice removed from reality. As spirits haunting New York in a novel they are, after all, only literary creations and so hover between the existence the reader grants them and the illusion the author asserts. At the end of *The Hothouse by the East River* Elsa and Paul stand in front of their apartment block. A new block is to be built on the site of the old. A Rolls-Royce drives up, bearing some friendly ghosts, and Elsa and Paul decide to join them, thus returning to the dead. The last sentence of the novel allows Elsa to depart with dignity as 'she trails her faithful and lithe cloud of unknowing across the pavement' (p. 140).

Throughout the three experimental novels the treatment of death is provocative. Spark takes free will and determinism to extraordinary artistic conclusions in *The Driver's Seat* and *Not to Disturb* and makes ghosts generate vitality in *The Hothouse by the East River*. Disbelieving in determinism, she nevertheless makes it part of her fictional formula in these three books; her paradoxical technique effortlessly accommodates a philosophical contradiction.

*

Once Elsa has caused a riot at her son's production of *Peter Pan*, the whimsical play within the fantasy of *The Hothouse by the East River*, the police arrive and Paul attempts to protect his family by revealing their unreality: 'Those people are not real. My son, my wife, my daughter, do not exist' (*HER*, p. 93). Odd characters do exist in Spark's fiction, but the factual figures she satirizes in her next novel are every bit as odd. Indeed some political developments in the USA must have seemed to Spark a God-given present of a plot. Spark's satire *The Abbess of Crewe* (1974) sets in an English abbey the scandal that eventually forced Richard Nixon to resign as President of the USA in 1974.

Although Nixon's massive majority over George McGovern in 1972 was a foregone conclusion, the Committee to Re-elect the President (Creep) indulged in dirty tricks, including the burglary of the Democratic Party headquarters in the Watergate complex in Washington. Nixon denied any prior knowledge of the break-in but was obviously implicated. Subsequently the presidential tapes revealed Nixon as a ruthless and often foul-mouthed operator determined to destroy his enemies. Nixon had made tapes of all his White House conversations and when he was compelled to release a transcript of these he had the expletives (and some crucial passages) deleted. In *The Abbess of Crewe*, Nixon's satirical representative also expurgates the transcripts of her taped conversations, putting 'Poetry deleted' (*AC*, p. 106) to account for the conspicuously absent sections of incriminating evidence.

The Nixonian figure in Spark's novel is Alexandra, who rises from Sub-Prioress to Abbess in an election campaign which she herself orchestrates. She puts electronic surveillance on her rival, Sister Felicity, who (like McGovern) 'wants everyone to be liberated by her vision and to acknowledge it' (p. 35). Aided by the trouble-shooting, globe-trotting Sister Gertrude (representing Nixon's Secretary of State Henry Kissinger) and abetted by sisters Mildred and Warburga (as John Ehrlichman and Bob Haldeman, Nixon's closest advisers), Alexandra encourages a plan to discredit Felicity. Two Jesuit novices break into the Abbey to steal love-letters from Felicity's work-box: this trial-run is discovered when Felicity notices her thimble is missing. When the scandal breaks Alexandra claims that the prestige of her position places her above everything: 'I know nothing about anything. I am occupied with the administration of the Abbey, our music, our rites and traditions, and our electronics project for contacts with our mission fields' (p. 90). With her arrogant mind closed within her 'white-skinned English skull' (p. 7) Alexandra is self-centred to the point of self-destruction – gifted yet ultimately idiotic in her abuse of personal power. John Updike has said that Spark 'does love [Alexandra] as she hasn't loved a character in a decade'[60] but the affection is for the character's charisma (a term much loved by American politicians), not for her corruption. The satire has its own internal morality.

'Nixon', said Bob Haldeman, the President's Chief of Staff at the White House, 'believed in miracles, which meant he believed in himself [because] he had always, miraculously, survived.'[61] The same might be said of Alexandra. Haldeman never saw *Nasty Habits* (1977), the film based on Spark's satire, but he did learn that the scenario (to use one of Alexandra's favourite expressions) takes place in a convent. It is the incongruity of the scenario that provides the comedy, the reader's expectations being overturned by the spectacle of intrigue in what passes for a centre of spiritual tranquillity. As in many of Spark's novels, appearance is deceptive. Alexandra, Mildred and Warburga look harmless – 'One white swan, two black, they file from the room' (*AC*, p. 28) – but they are skilled exponents of electronic bugging. In the Abbess of Crewe's parlour is an image of the Infant of Prague, but this precious relic plays a part in the ecclesiastical conspiracy:

> The Abbess reaches out to the Infant of Prague and touches with the tip of her finger a ruby embedded in its vestments. After a space she speaks: 'The motorway from London to Crewe is jammed with reporters, according to the news. The A51 is a solid mass of vehicles. In the midst of the strikes and the oil crises.' (p. 18)

She is systematically recording her comments.

Told in the present tense (like the experimental novels *The Driver's Seat*, *Not to Disturb* and *The Hothouse by the East River*), with an expository first chapter prefacing a narrative flashback, the satire extracts the maximum of humour by mocking the heroic pretensions of the Nixon administration. Before and after the 'third-rate burglary' (p. 74) Sister Gertrude is eternally elsewhere in her helicopter, concerning herself with 'ecclesiastical ephemera' (p. 23) in Africa or Asia while the convent is 'a hotbed of corruption and hypocrisy' (p. 49) and Rome burns with moral indignation. The husky voice of Henry Kissinger is given to Gertrude, who therefore sounds bronchial over the telephone. Gertrude's advice to Alexandra is both dire and diplomatic: 'Consult Machiavelli. A great master, but don't quote me as saying so; the name is inexpedient' (p. 44).

The conversational crudity of Richard Nixon is occasionally attributed to Alexandra and contrasts with her fondness for quoting poems. Thinking of Sister Felicity's affair with Thomas the Jesuit, Alexandra observes: 'I must say a Jesuit, or any priest for that matter, would be the last man I would myself elect to be laid by. A man who undresses, maybe; but one who unfrocks, no' (p. 20). Still, her plans to reorganize the Abbey will ensure that

'The nuns will have each her Jesuit' (p. 47), and she tells two Jesuit Fathers that 'your brother-Jesuit Thomas has taken to screwing our sister Felicity by night under the poplars' (p. 54). The poplars are, of course, bugged; intimate encounters are recorded in the control room, 'where spools, spools and spools twirl obediently for hours and many hours' (p. 68).

Sex plays a part in the comedy throughout *The Abbess of Crewe*. The Jesuits who steal Felicity's silver thimble are guilty of penetrating her privacy, though Alexandra denies that the thimble is a sexual symbol. When sister Winifrede deposits Alexandra's hush money in the ladies' lavatory on the ground floor at Selfridge's there is comic relief since the woman who picks up the cash is a Jesuit novice dressed in drag. 'It is', Alexandra complains, 'typical of the Jesuit mentality to complicate a simple process' (p. 88). Symbolically, in a fine set-piece during which Alexandra lectures her nuns on the pitfalls of bourgeois morality, Felicity takes out her embroidery frame and attacks 'the piece of stuff with her accurate and ever-piercing needle . . . stabs and stabs again, as it might be to draw blood' (p. 73). Described by Alexandra as 'a lascivious puritan' (p. 94), Sister Felicity dreams of creating a 'love-Abbey . . . a love-nest' (p. 40), but goes on television to confess to the masses that she is undergoing psychiatric treatment after being excommunicated for living in sin with Thomas the Jesuit. The nuns, the silent majority in the convent, accept what is put before them, unaware that their diet includes catfood and dogfood as well as hypocrisy.

Ironically, Alexandra dismisses the convent crisis as trivial, certain that 'Such a scandal could never arise in the United States of America' (p. 19). Alexandra is truly corrupt in her conviction that foul means justify a selfish end. If Spark sympathizes with her it is because Alexandra has the egotism of the artist, adamant that she has a right to compel others into acting out the drama of her destiny. Alexandra believes (catastrophically as it turns out) that appearance can conceal truth; her failure is her inability to fulfil honourably the demands of her self-imposed destiny. She leaves the novel by sailing to Rome and contemplating 'how the wide sea billows from shore to shore like that cornfield of sublimity which never should be reaped nor was ever sown, orient and immortal

101

wheat' (p. 107). Her vision, according to the logic of Spark's satire, has been distorted by the sin of pride.

As a satirist Spark uses poetic precedents ranging from Dryden to Eliot. Not for her the hyperbolic savagery, the verbal overkill, of Swift or Wyndham Lewis. Instead, in *The Abbess of Crewe* she does as Dryden, in *Absalom and Achitophel* (1681), did before her; she establishes religious parallels for the politically powerful and presents them in an exquisitely textured work. In *The Ballad of Peckham Rye* Spark combined the influence of the traditional ballad with references to Eliot's *The Waste Land*. In *The Abbess of Crewe*, Eliot's modernism coexists with Dryden's neo-classicism.

Like Dryden, Spark sustains the satire through an intelligent attention to details. But *The Abbess of Crewe* is not only poetic in its satiric tone, for the entire text is organized like a modernist sequence. Ecclesiastical allusions are juxtaposed against poetic quotations, discursive sections are set against lyrical interludes, fantasy is counterpointed with farce. After a factual passage about systems of recorded sound the nuns incongruously utter 'Amen', then Spark lifts her prose to another level:

> The Abbess of Crewe's parlour glows with bright ornaments and brightest of all is a two-foot statue of the Infant of Prague. The Infant is adorned with its traditional robes, the episcopal crown and vestments embedded with such large and so many rich and gleaming jewels it would seem they could not possibly be real. (*AC*, p. 15)

The glow and the jewels were prompted by 'A Game of Chess' in *The Waste Land*. Certainly Spark's abrupt changes of narrative mood, her swift transitions between everyday and exalted modes of language, her combination of ritual and romance are all reminiscent of Eliot's great poem. The constructional principles of *The Waste Land* have not been lost on Spark. She has assembled *The Abbess of Crewe* as a modernist work of satire. As an amalgam of special compositional effects it is a highly effective scenario and, as the Abbess of Crewe says of scenarios, 'They are an art form based on facts. A good scenario is a garble. A bad one is a bungle. They need not be plausible, only hypnotic, like all good art' (p. 89).

*

102

Though not so specifically satirical as *The Abbess of Crewe*, Spark's next two novels are highly critical in tone, taking modern Italy – the heartland of the Roman Catholic religion – as a country of moral chaos. Faith, in *The Takeover* (1976) and *Territorial Rights* (1979), has only a face value. Moreover, this face has farcical features. Technically there is an enormous verve in the two novels, Spark being consummately in control of her craft and utterly confident of her artistic powers. Both novels are extremely polished performances, clearly the creations of a verbal virtuoso.

There is a comic-operatic quality about *The Takeover*, a novel set in the years 1973–5, for all the intricacies of plot are designed to seem stranger than the average fiction. Maggie Radcliffe, the apparently indestructible and immensely wealthy heroine, takes as her third husband an Italian marquis, Adalberto di Tullio-Friole, yet sleeps with her servant Lauro, whose criminal connections eventually save her from financial catastrophe. Hubert Mallindaine, who lives in one of Maggie's three houses at Nemi, is 'a confirmed queer' (*T*, p. 77) and pagan who depends on the devotion of his adoring secretary Pauline Thin, a Roman Catholic. Secondary characters include two Jesuit priests, Father Cuthbert Plaice and Father Gerard Harvey, fascinated by Hubert's cult of Diana of Nemi; Coco de Renault, an Argentinian financier who appropriates Maggie's fortune; Massimo de Vita, a lawyer who exploits the asininity of Italian law; two elegant art thieves, Malcolm Stuyvesant and George Falk, who are obligingly given a tour of the Villa Tullio by Maggie's unsuspecting husband.

It is established early in the novel that the 1970s represent the end of an era, a notion conveyed by comical means. The radio announces the death of Noël Coward, and Hubert reflects platitudinously that 'Eras pass. . . . They pass every day' (p. 10). Hubert is certain of his own survival, for he has a false faith: he claims to be the direct descendant of the goddess Diana of Nemi. Spark undermines Hubert's false faith by inserting into the novel a long quotation (pp. 40–1) from J. G. Frazer's *The Golden Bough* (1890–1915), a work blessed by T. S. Eliot in the notes to *The Waste Land*. Hubert's proximity to the panorama of Nemi, the lake, the lush vegetation, 'the scene which had stirred the imagination of Sir James Frazer' (p. 8), is 'suddenly . . . too expensive'

103

(p. 9). Conscious that he cannot forever afford the luxury of Nemi, Hubert meditates on the meaning of his life. His confusion is described by Spark in a passage that contrasts poetic fancy with a chemical fact of modern life:

> Where is the poetry of my life? Hubert thought. He retained an inkling that the poetry was still there and would return. Wordsworth defined poetry as 'emotion recollected in tranquillity'. Hubert took a tranquillizer, quite a mild one called Mitgil, and knew he would feel better in about ten minutes. To make sure, he took another. (p. 10)

Hubert's plan to restore his own financial fortunes as well as the cult of Diana confirm him as a fake sustained by false faith; a fake in a fraudulent world. In the house he has obtained from Maggie the Louis XIV chairs have been replaced by 'very beautiful fakes' (p. 104), the Gauguin has been replaced by a copy. His plans to replace a Corot with a fake are thwarted by a typical Sparkian irony, for the experts inform him that the Corot is already a fake, 'an expensive fake, but not marketable enough to have copied' (p. 105). It emerges during the narrative that Maggie's property at Nemi has been built on fraudulent foundations, for the lawyer Massimo discovers that the building permit was a fake: 'The whole of the transaction had been a fake, including the documents' (p. 135). Far from belonging to Maggie, the land at Nemi is the property of Elisabetta, the fiancée of Maggie's sexually voracious servant Lauro. Though he has been successively servant to Hubert, then Maggie's son, then Maggie, Lauro ends the novel as the mercenary master of the situation. He arranges for Maggie's fraudulent financier Coco de Renault to be kidnapped by the Mafia, claiming 30 per cent of the pay-off.

As the various characters interact and plot against each other like the cast of an *opera buffa*, the insecure state of the world makes their absurdity appropriate to the era of the 1970s. The Middle East War of 1973 coincides with Hubert's creation of a new religion; the electoral success of the Italian Communists in 1975 comes at a time when millionairess Maggie faces financial ruin. The international oil-trauma has 'inaugurated the Dark Ages II' (*T*, p. 99), and burglary, blackmail, kidnap and bogus religion are endemic in Italy. Even the Roman Catholic Church is unsteady as it absorbs the impact of the Charismatic Renewal Movement; at Hubert's gathering of the Friends of Diana the two Jesuit priests significantly give out 'charismatic smiles in all directions' (p. 156).

Throughout *The Takeover*, faith has been replaced by fraud. Italy, the birthplace of *opera buffa*, is a land in which excitement is generated by absurdity. The notion of excitement is crucial to the novel – Spark uses the term like a recurring musical motif. Father Cuthbert Plaice, discussing Catholicism with Pauline (note the Christian name) Thin, is seen 'shifting about with excitement in his chair as if he were sexually as much as pastorally aroused' (p. 12). Lauro, on discovering Elisabetta's claim to Nemi, is 'excited by the surprising idea that she had so much land of her own' (p. 134). The lawyer Massimo, learning that Maggie has no legal rights to Nemi, 'looked excited' (p. 135). Hubert finds the oddity of Italian law 'very exciting' (p. 137). Describing a meeting of the Charismatic Renewal Movement, Pauline says 'everybody was excited' (p. 151). At the climactic meeting of Hubert's congregation, Letizia, 'a passionate Italian nationalist with an ardour for folklore and the voluntary helping of youthful drug-addicts' (p. 23), behaves 'excitedly' (p. 162). Authentic religious ecstasy, in *The Takeover*, has been replaced by egocentric excitement.

It is the excited atmosphere of Hubert's faithful, the Friends of Diana, on a hot day towards the end of June, that most fully engages Spark's comedic attention. She reduces the pagan sublime to the utterly ridiculous. Hubert, decked out in silver–green priestly vestments, is appalled at the appearance of his secretary Pauline in a khaki cotton trouser-suit with metal-gold buttons on the coat, her trouser-legs tucked into a pair of high canvas boots. 'You look', Hubert tells Pauline, 'like the commandant of a concentration camp or something out of a London brothel' (p. 153). However, the show must go on, and the throng gathers from a combination of motives, having in common a capacity for excitement. Hubert, standing in his leafy bower, speaks as the direct descendant of the goddess Diana, 'Diana of Nemi, Diana of the Woods and so, indirectly, of her brother the god Apollo' (p. 156). Hubert takes himself seriously but inadvertently acts the fool.

Hubert's pagan flow is interrupted by Pauline, who grabs the loudspeaker and reads a biblical passage to demonstrate that some words of the Apostle Paul refer to Diana of Ephesus, a revelation that enthuses Nancy Cowan, an English tutor about to marry a rich Italian. She attacks Hubert, an act that introduces a set-piece of rich farce:

> Nancy was fairly strong, but Hubert now had her by the hair. His sleeve was half torn off. Presently Letizia excitedly came to help Nancy in whatever role she was playing; she was probably drawn to the girl's assistance by the fact that she felt in conflict about Hubert, disliking him personally but fascinated by his nature cult. The sound of hand-clapping mounted again, all round the fighters; Letizia was fairly carried away, so that, in passing, having drawn blood from Hubert's cheeks with her nails she frenziedly tore off her own blouse under which she wore nothing. She fought on, topless, while Nancy concentrated on tearing the green and shining robes piece by piece from Hubert's back. . . . The two priests stood some way from that throne and scene of battle, exhorting frantically. Cuthbert came a little too close and received a casual swipe from Hubert which sent him to the ground. Soon the clothes were torn from the Jesuits, and in fact everyone in the garden was involved in the riot within a very short time. (*T*, p. 162)

Nature has been invoked by Hubert and arrives red in tooth and claw.

Following the riot, three of Hubert's homosexual secretaries come to kill him at the command of Maggie, but cannot carry out the assassination. This absurd scene is followed by Maggie's use of Lauro to kidnap Coco de Renault and thus regain the money he has swindled from her. The contemporary god of money is seemingly triumphant. As the novel ends Hubert and Pauline prepare to leave Nemi. Hubert walks towards the temple of Diana and meets Maggie, dressed symbolically in rags. They have both adapted to the new era with their sense of survival, if not their honour, intact. They part as friends, though for most of the book Maggie has been trying to eject Hubert from Nemi. They agree that, in a crooked world, 'There are times when one can trust a crook' (p. 189). The final paragraph indicates, in richly lyrical prose, that the ruthless Maggie is the modern equivalent of the pagan goddess Diana:

> She said good night very sweetly and, lifting her dingy skirts, picked her way along the leafy path, hardly needing her flashlamp, so bright was the moon, three-quarters full, illuminating the lush lakeside and, in the fields beyond, the kindly fruits of the earth.

In going back to nature Maggie has the measure of her own nature. She has her faith in a faithless world, she understands why her contemporaries are content to sacrifice their principles.

*

Territorial Rights, like *The Takeover*, is an intricately plotted novel and it too comments ironically on the absurdity of incidents that seem integral to modern Italy. In a telephone call from Venice to Anthea Leaver in Birmingham, Grace Gregory – retired matron of Ambrose College, where Anthea's husband Arnold had been headmaster – reports back on some of the strange relationships she has witnessed. She assures her friend, 'It may seem far-fetched to you, Anthea, but here everything is stark realism. This is Italy' (*TR*, p. 127). *Territorial Rights* uses the starkly realistic texture of a thriller in which odd actions invariably speak louder than the words of the participants in the plot. All the characters interlock in the interests of a 'far-fetched' scenario which Spark presents as plausible in an Italian context. Whereas Thomas Mann wrote pessimistically about death in Venice, Spark touches mischievously on life in Venice.

Robert Leaver, son of Anthea and Arnold, is a 24-year-old student who travels from Paris to Venice ostensibly to study the architecture of Santa Maria Formosa. Actually he is aggrieved by the memory of being treated with some contempt in Paris by Mark Curran (always known simply by his surname), an American multi-millionaire art collector and painter. Robert arrives in Venice in October and books into the Pensione Sofia owned by the sisters Eufemia and Katerina. Looking through the window of his room, Robert notices that the sisters each have an equal share of the Pensione Sofia's garden, which is dotted with rose-beds and divided by a gravel pathway itself further divided by a row of whitewashed stones. Since Spark does not include insignificant details in her novels this bipartisan arrangement is obviously important.

Robert's presence in Venice activates the others. He is reunited with Curran, who has come to Venice 'to settle things with Robert' (*TR*, p. 12). He also meets his father, who is in Venice with his mistress Mary Tiller, but Arnold Leaver is so embarrassed by this encounter that he moves from the Pensione Sofia to the Hotel Lord Byron, where Curran is in residence. Robert's third relationship in Venice is with the artist Lina Pancev, a defector from Communist Bulgaria who hopes to find the grave of her father in Venice. Eleven years older than Robert, Lina is, as Arnold Leaver observes approvingly, 'a bright-eyed ... full-fledged and juicy young woman' (p. 146). She is also eccentric, disposing of her domestic debris in the streets in a novel manner: 'Then she bent to lift her voluminous skirt to the knees, and shook out from under it an empty mackerel-tin, a milk-carton, bits of egg-shell and some pieces of old lettuce' (p. 9). Spark completes her cast of primary characters by introducing the Countess Violet de Winter, a widow living in Ca' Winter, a large palace on the Grand Canal. At the suggestion of Curran, Violet gives Lina Pancev a job as an au pair and offers an attic for use as a studio. The participants in Spark's involved plot begin to impinge on each other.

Intrigue, in Spark's novel, is an international affair. Back in England, Anthea Leaver goes to Coventry to consult Mr B., an executive of the private investigation agency GESS (Global-Equip Security Services). She wants the dirt on her husband's trip with Mary Tiller and is willing to pay a price for scurrilous information, though Mr B. warns that his investigation could be expensive: 'We have to send a man abroad to consult with our expert on the spot. . . . We have no territorial rights. Expenses here, expenses there, they mount up' (p. 44). Mr B.'s motives are mercenary to an extraordinary degree, for GESS is no ordinary security firm but a business built on blackmail, using its inside knowledge to extract payments from those under investigation. Violet de Winter, Spark explains, also works for GESS as its chief agent in Northern Italy and she realizes she can use Lina Pancev to obtain essential information for the firm. Venice is a moral vacuum which the characters fill with vice.

Robert, an amoral opportunist who has been a prostitute in Paris, is in his element in Venice, where his own schemes inadvertently assist the criminal cause of GESS. Teaming up with the butcher Giorgio and his niece Anna, Robert decides to extract 'big money' (p. 168) from Curran. He contrives a dramatic disappearance and writes to Curran claiming he has been kidnapped and will be released for 'Several million dollars' (p. 103). Robert advances Spark's plot by uncovering information that threatens various characters. He suspects that Curran and Violet have been German agents during the Second World War and that Lina's father, Victor Pancev, has been murdered. Moreover, Robert's 'notes for a novel' (p. 107) – fiction and fact attracting his attention equally, as is customary with a Spark creation – reveal that Katerina and Eufemia, illegitimate daughters of the Count de Winter, were both so 'madly in love' (p. 116) with Victor Pancev that a 'fascist butcher' (p. 117) was employed to cut his dead body in two to ensure that the two bits could be buried on both sides of their garden. Robert's friend Giorgio was the apprentice who helped the fascist butcher to cut Victor Pancev's body in two.

Through Violet, Curran does a deal with Mr B. of GESS, paying him half a million dollars for immunity. Giorgio, realizing that his outfit cannot compete with the professional blackmailers of GESS, makes the best of a bad job and advises Robert and Anna to leave Venice, which they do, taking to robbery and earning the title 'I Bonnie e Clyde d'Italia' (p. 183). From these elements Spark contrives a parody of the happy ending, for Robert and Anna gladly go to the Middle East to train as terrorists, Anthea is happy when Robert sends a stolen diamond and sapphire bracelet to her Birmingham home, Lina returns to Bulgaria where she is 'put to happy use as a first-rate example of a repentant dissident' (p. 187), Curran travels to India to see his guru, Violet launches a tourist project called 'Venice by Night' (p. 187), Arnold Leaver returns to Birmingham to find his wife 'in good humour' (p. 188), Grace Gregory and Mary Tiller go on a round-the-world tour together, Katerina and Eufemia cultivate roses in the garden that contains the divided remains of Victor Pancev. The self-deception and corruption of the characters in *Territorial Rights* are condemned by the author's expert use of irony.

Lina Pancev, for example, provides three ingeniously ironic moments in the novel. Asked to do some shopping for Violet, she answers, 'I know good butchery when I see it' (p. 92) and goes to Giorgio's shop innocent of the fact that this good butcher has helped to carve up her father's body. An anti-Semite, Lina is horrified when she discovers that Leo, to whom she makes love, is the son of a Cockney Jewish mother, and she jumps into the canal to rid herself of racial contamination; she then has to go to bed with antibiotics against possible infection from the canal waters. Out one evening with Arnold Leaver, Lina decides to dance and at the Pensione Sofia is told that Robert wants her to dance in the centre rose-beds, first the far one, then the near one. By doing this Lina is, of course, dancing on her father's grave – or rather graves, as his remains are equally divided.

*

Perhaps the experience of commenting so caustically on her adopted Italy in *The Takeover* and *Territorial Rights* made Spark look back with affection to the formative years she spent in London before she became a famous novelist. *Loitering with Intent* (1981), her most affirmative autobiographical novel, offers variations on some earlier themes. More precisely, the way the novel examines the nature of fictional truth makes *Loitering with Intent* a mature variant on *The Comforters*. Like that first novel, *Loitering with Intent* deals with a decisive period in Spark's evolution as a creative writer. A first-personal performance (as was *Robinson*), *Loitering with Intent* purports to be an autobiographical account of the years 1949–50 when the narrator was a young woman in London and conscious of 'what a wonderful thing it was to be a woman and an artist in the twentieth century' (*LI*, p. 129).

Fleur Talbot, who tells the tale, describes the genesis of her first novel *Warrender Chase*; Caroline Rose, in *The Comforters*, was actively involved in writing her first novel. Fleur lives, as did Caroline, in Queen's Gate, and, like Caroline, is a 'Catholic believer' (p. 92). Whereas Caroline was initially confused by the creative process, Fleur is confidently in control of her autobiographical text, which is full of assertive asides on the nature of the novel: 'Contradictions in human nature are one of its most consistent notes [so] to make a character ring true it needs must be in some way contradictory, somewhere a paradox' (p. 30). Paradoxically, Fleur is offering her own autobiography as fact, though she has good reason to doubt the veracity of most memoirs. On its scintillating surface *Loitering with Intent* is an autobiography by a woman who has lost her faith in autobiography as a meaningful form.

While working on her first novel, Fleur gets a job as secretary to Sir Quentin Oliver, founder of the Autobiographical Association, whose members are required to produce memoirs which are retained by Sir Quentin and supposedly shelved for seventy years in order to protect the living. Given the task of typing up the members' memoirs, Fleur is bored until she discovers a way of making her work bearable: 'I hit on the method of making [the memoirs] expertly worse; and everyone concerned was delighted with the result' (p. 23). By making their characters more colourful, more contradictory, Fleur appeals to the egocentricity of the memoirists: 'I had set them writing fictions about themselves' (p. 83). For them, Fleur's fictional inventions are more satisfying than their factual confessions. Extending the fiction-within-a-fiction format of *The Comforters* Spark compels her autobiographical heroine to operate in an area where fact, fiction and fantasy are interchangeable.

Fleur says of her own fictional hero, 'Warrender Chase never existed, he is only some hundreds of words, some punctuation, sentences, paragraphs, marks on the page' (p. 61). So are all created characters in a novel, whether that novel be Fleur's *Warrender Chase* or Spark's *Loitering with Intent*. Just as she did in *The Comforters*, Spark is playing conceptual games with the reader's perception of truth. When Sir Quentin quotes 'the old adage, Truth is stronger than Fiction' (p. 14), Fleur merely acknowledges the existence of the saying. As a novelist she knows that fiction can be stranger than truth. In one of her asides Fleur says, 'When I first started writing people used to say my novels

111

were exaggerated. They never were exaggerated, merely aspects of realism' (p. 64). The remark is far from innocent, especially as it occurs in a novel treating truth as a fictional form; for Spark reality is rooted in the imagination of the artist, not in the physical facts of life.

Fleur's eponymous hero Warrender Chase is apparently an eminent man, an 'ambassador-poet and moralist' (p. 44). Her novel, however, exposes him as 'privately a sado-puritan who for a kind of hobby had gathered together a group of people specially selected for their weakness and folly, and in whom he carefully planted and nourished a sense of terrible and unreal guilt' (pp. 59–60). Warrender is helped by his housekeeper Charlotte, 'that English Rose' (p. 61), and his nephew Roland's wife Marjorie. Warrender also has an ancient mother, Prudence. As Fleur mingles with Sir Quentin and the members of his Autobiographical Association, she feels that human nature tends to copy her art for the characters she meets increasingly conform to the types she has introduced into her fiction. Thus the usual routine of writing is reversed for Fleur Talbot. 'Sometimes,' confides Fleur, 'I don't actually meet a character I have created in a novel until some time after the novel has been written and published' (p. 19). There Fleur speaks directly for Muriel Spark, who told Malcolm Muggeridge in an interview, 'sometimes I invent a character that I meet later on after the book is written.'[62]

Having fixed the characters Warrender Chase, Charlotte, Marjorie and Prudence in her fiction, Fleur compares them to their actual counterparts – though Fleur's actuality is, paradoxically, Spark's fiction. Sir Quentin, a 'psychological Jack the Ripper' (p. 44), corresponds to Warrender; Beryl Tims, Sir Quentin's odious housekeeper, to Charlotte; Dottie Carpenter, wife of Fleur's lover Leslie, to Marjorie; Lady Edwina, Sir Quentin's eccentric mother, to Prudence. Just as Warrender Chase, a biblical fundamentalist, imposes his will (which he identifies with God's) on the members of his prayer-set, so Sir Quentin becomes a 'mad spiritual leader' (p. 138) who controls the members of the Autobiographical Association. He not only exerts moral blackmail by abusing the guilty secrets they have recorded in their memoirs, he doses them with Dexedrine. All the members of the Autobiographical Association are insecure and psychologically unsettled: for example, Maisie Young, crippled in an accident, regards herself as 'a cripple and a bore' (p. 68); Father Egbert Delaney is an unfrocked priest; Lady Bernice Gilbert has a lesbian past; Mrs Wilks has a paranoid fear of being assassinated by Trotskyite agents; the Baronne Clotilde du Loiret is 'stunned by privilege' (p. 138). Compared to them, Lady Edwina – indiscreet and incontinent – is normal, and features as the most loveable figure in the book.

In *Loitering with Intent* fact and fiction coexist uneasily. By her own admission, Fleur is an extremely neurotic novelist. In one fit of temper she tears up Dottie's memoir, in another she tears up some pages of her own manuscript. She is 'paranoiac' (p. 87), in 'a state of anxiety' (p. 94), 'hysterical' (p. 126), 'tight-strung' (p. 129), 'depressed' (p. 144). She completes *Warrender Chase* while suffering from flu; so just as Caroline Rose, in *The Comforters*, heard voices which she subsequently identified as the sound of her own dictation, Fleur writes *Warrender Chase* in a frenetic fury of creativity. Spark hints that her heroine is capable of confusing fact and fiction, subconsciously as well as consciously, for Fleur recalls a time when she 'sat and wondered if I were going mad, if *Warrender Chase* existed or had I imagined the book' (p. 88). When she considers how Sir Quentin is assuming the role of Warrender Chase she says, 'I could have invented him' (p. 75) and 'I almost feel I invented him' (p. 80). To underline this ambiguity, this interdependence of fact and fiction, Fleur's friend Wally tells her 'Sometimes . . . you're suddenly not *there*' (p. 145). The reader is reminded how Georgina Hogg, in *The Comforters*, disappears when not perceived by the author. Fleur Talbot, founded in autobiographical fact, remains a figment of Muriel Spark's imagination. Fiction is a literary, not necessarily a literal, fact.

Varying the epistolary device of an exchange of letters, Spark tightens her plot with a series of stolen papers. Sir Quentin, convinced that *Warrender Chase* is 'an attempted *roman à clef* if ever there was one' (p. 131), has Dottie steal Fleur's manuscript and the putative publisher of *Warrender Chase* distribute the type and destroy the proofs of the printed text. As a reprisal Fleur steals the papers of the Autobiographical Association to exert pressure on her adversary (so getting to grips with Warrender

Chase's original or imitator, depending on which role best suits Sir Quentin). Fleur recovers her novel, Sir Quentin regains the papers of the Autobiographical Association, nature continues to copy art. Warrender has encouraged a woman to commit suicide, so Sir Quentin inflicts the same fate on Lady Bernice; Warrender is killed in a car crash, Sir Quentin suffers the same fate. Fleur accepts all this as aesthetically inevitable, secure in the knowledge that she is 'an artist, not a reporter' (p. 109) and that her odd experiences will thereafter inform her art: 'In fact, under one form or another, whether I have liked it or not, I have written about [Sir Quentin and his set] ever since, the straws from which I have made my bricks' (p. 142).

Fleur's joy at being an artist and a woman in the twentieth century is conveyed in the anecdote that opens the book and reappears at the beginning of the final chapter. On the last day of June 1950, Fleur is eating sandwiches in an old Kensington graveyard when a young policeman asks her what she is up to, pointing out that she could be guilty of 'loitering with intent' (p. 143). That, she realizes, is the nature of her art, a habit of purposively haunting the earth while possessed by creative vitality. When Dottie sees that Fleur has become a successful novelist with a story uncannily like the saga of Sir Quentin, she accuses Fleur of 'having plotted and planned it all', and Fleur agrees that she has been 'loitering with intent' (p. 156). That is the creative role Spark has relished, enriching everyday reality with art. Fleur's autobiography is a fiction but also an actual work of art that conveys its own integrity. In this sense it is deliberately compared to two classic autobiographies, Benvenuto Cellini's *La Vita* (posthumously published in 1728) and Newman's *Apologia pro Vita Sua* (1864). For Fleur, Newman's book is 'a beautiful piece of poetic paranoia' (p. 70), while Cellini's work is 'sheer magic' (p. 88), showing how the artist 'enjoyed a long love affair with his art' (p. 89). Spark's own love affair with the art of fiction is the emotional crux of *Loitering with Intent*, which is why she closes it joyfully: 'And so, having entered the fullness of my years, from there by the grace of God I go on my way rejoicing' (p. 158).

*

Loitering with Intent restates, in an infinitely more relaxed style than *The Comforters*, the fact-as-fiction subject-matter of Spark's first novel. *The Only Problem* (1984) reaches back to a theological issue implicit in *The Comforters* whose title refers to the Book of Job, a work cited only once in that first novel. As Caroline Rose, heroine of *The Comforters*, approaches Brompton Oratory she is intimidated by its appearance, finding it an oppressively 'big monster of a place' (p. 111). Whenever she enters 'a line from the Book of Job came to her mind, "Behold nŏw Behemoth which I made with thee"' (p. 111). In 1953 Spark was working on a book about the Book of Job,[63] and in an article published in 1955 she said that Job:

> not only argues the problem of suffering, he suffers the problem of argument. . . . [Job is] surrounded by a conspiracy of mediocrity, obsessed with a raging need to shock [the comforters] and at the same time to communicate his feelings. . . . [Dialogue in the Book of Job] makes no rational progress [for] the characters cannot understand each other.[64]

Spark has also joked that she could improve on 'points of characterization and philosophy'[65] in the Book of Job, a text that 'will never come clear [which] doesn't matter, it's a poem,' as Harvey Gotham claims in *The Only Problem* (*OP*, p. 132).

The Only Problem is the outcome of Spark's many years of thinking about the Book of Job. 'How can you deal with the problem of suffering if everybody conspires to estrange you from suffering?' (p. 64); that is a question pertinently posed by Harvey Gotham, a Canadian millionaire in his mid-thirties. For the only problem, according to Harvey, is what theologians call theodicy: God's tolerance of human misery in a world he created in his own image. Harvey, says Spark:

> could not face that a benevolent Creator, one whose charming and delicious light descended and spread over the world, and being powerful everywhere, could condone the unspeakable sufferings of the world; that God did permit all suffering and was therefore by logic of his omnipotence, the actual author of it, he was at a loss how to square with the existence of God, given the premise that God is good.

'It is the only problem,' Harvey had always said. Now, Harvey believed in God, and this was what tormented him. 'It's the only problem, in fact, worth discussing.' (p. 19)

The only problem, in fact – or in Spark's mature fiction.

Harvey sets out to solve the only problem by composing a monograph on the Book of Job. He settles in the Vosges, France, after visiting Epinal to look at George de la Tour's painting 'Job Visited by his Wife' in the museum there. As the novel opens Harvey is ensconced in his French cottage, insulated from the everyday problems that overwhelm other people. He has money, time on his hands and a sense of his own intellectual importance. His self-centred serenity is disturbed when a visitor calls. Harvey's brother-in-law Edward Jansen, an actor, brings with him details of the domestic life that Harvey has tried to leave behind him. It is established that Harvey left his wife Effie because he disapproved of her stealing two bars of chocolate on an Italian holiday. What disturbed Harvey was Effie's insistence that her theft was a politically significant gesture. 'Why shouldn't we help ourselves?', Effie had asked Harvey: 'These multinationals and monopolies are capitalising on us, and two-thirds of the world is suffering' (*OP*, p. 15). The pattern begins to cohere for, characteristically, Spark is working on several levels simultaneously, satirizing the ability of intellectuals to rationalize their antisocial impulses while also putting the biblical notion of suffering into a contemporary setting.

In the Old Testament, Job is, so God tells Satan, 'a perfect and an upright man, one that feareth God, and escheweth evil' (Job 1: 8). After being smitten with boils, as a test of his spiritual sincerity, he is plagued by the comforters and advised by his wife to 'curse God, and die' (Job 2: 9). Job, however, holds firm to his faith in divine justice, despite evidence to the contrary. Harvey, in the first part of the novel, is more fortunate than Job in that he is not so suddenly thrust into an appalling situation. Commercially he is as secure as Job, who was a man of great substance; Harvey has inherited a vast share of a Canadian uncle's fortune. His money buys him legal advice and instantly solves practical problems. His insight into Job's predicament is an intellectual affectation.

Harvey's wife Effie, who is off-stage for most of the fictional

116

drama, wants alimony from Harvey – a desire which she feels is consistent with her political philosophy of relieving capitalists of their capital. Harvey, however, wishes to have nothing to do with Effie and leaves her to her own devices. He is, though, interested in her child by another man, so Effie's sister Ruth Jansen brings the baby Clara to France. Ruth settles down with Harvey and even discusses the meaning of the Book of Job·with him, since he is still struggling, philosophically, with the only problem that interests him. Harvey eschews evil only because it has never visited him. Ruth genuinely comforts him, as does the baby. When Ruth decides that the three of them need a bigger house, Harvey buys a chateau half a mile from his cottage. He is content, and even the news that Effie has been arrested for shoplifting in a Trieste supermarket simply confirms his view of her as a kleptomaniac he can well do without.

The novel erupts into action in Part Two. Just as Job had to suffer for his faith, so Harvey is plagued by a sudden series of misfortunes, troubled by events beyond his control. A terrorist group, the FLE (Front for the Liberation of Europe), has committed a series of crimes in the Vosges. As Harvey discovers, the police are convinced that the leader of the FLE is none other than his wife Effie. Harvey is interrogated by police officers and – adding journalistic insult to ethical injury – caricatured in the newspapers as The Guru of the Vosges, an American prophet 'inveighing against God, who he claims has unjustly condemned the world to suffering' (*OP*, p. 123). When a policeman is murdered in Paris, Effie is the main suspect, a situation that encourages Harvey to indulge in abstract thought rather than action:

> Do I suffer on Effie's account? Yes, and perhaps I can live by that experience. We all need something to suffer about. But *Job*, my work on *Job*, all interrupted and neglected, probed into and interfered with: that is experience, too; real experience, not vicarious, as is often assumed. To study, to think, is to live and suffer painfully.
>
> Did Effie really kill or help to kill the policeman in Paris whose wife was shopping in the suburbs at the time? . . . Yes, he could imagine Effie in the scene; she was capable of that, capable of anything. (p. 154)

117

Harvey (like Job) accepts his ordeal philosophically. He is, like several Spark protagonists, self-centred to the point of solipsism. Everything that occurs is grist to his mill.

Spark extracts both hilarity and horror from the biblical parallels in *The Only Problem*. When the news of Effie's alleged part in the murder of a policeman reaches Canada, Harvey's Auntie Pet leaves Toronto to comfort him in France. The information that Auntie Pet brings, however, is hardly calculated to reassure Harvey: she says that she knows Effie could not have killed the policeman since she was in California at the time appearing on Canadian television during a documentary on hippy communes. Auntie Pet is adamant when Harvey questions her story, telling him

> I ought to recognize Effie when I see her. She was naked, with her hair hanging down her shoulders, and laughing, and then pulling her consort after her out of the extra-marital bag, without shame; I am truly sorry, Harvey, to be the bearer of this news. To a Gotham. Better she killed a policeman. It's a question of honour. Mind you, I always suspected she was unvirtuous. (p. 172)

Harvey understands Auntie Pet's logic, admitting to himself that he would rather think of Effie as a terrorist than as a sexually promiscuous member of a commune.

In the minuscule third part of *The Only Problem*, Spark recalls Job's just reward and ironically asserts that Harvey's tragedy is 'that of the happy ending' (p. 186). Harvey has completed his monograph on the Book of Job and solved the only problem to his own intellectual satisfaction. Tragically, however, suffering persists as a fact of life, though he refuses to recognize it as relevant to his own life. The police, after massacring the terrorist gang in Paris, ask Harvey to identify the body of his dead wife. When he sees her he feels she looks 'more than ever like Job's wife' (p. 186) and he finds it impossible to acknowledge that the death of Effie means the destruction of his academic ideal: 'Yes, but this isn't my wife. . . . Yes, it's my wife, Effie' (p. 187).

Harvey is an intellectual who has rejected reality in the interests of his academic isolationism. His vision of a suitable wife is inspired by George de la Tour's painting where 'the painter was idealizing some notion of his own [as] Job and his wife are deeply in love' (p. 78). Unable to possess the painted image Harvey settles for Ruth, Effie's sister, for she too looks like George de la Tour's artistic impression of Job's wife. Harvey looks forward to playing the part of Job; his ambition is to live 'another hundred and forty years [and] have three daughters, Clara, Jemima and Eye-Paint' (p. 189). Harvey is content to live with his fantasies concerning Job's wife, but he is a hero divorced from the reality that informs Spark's work. That reality, as Spark makes plain in her paradoxical manner, demands an act of genuine faith in the truth of her fiction.

*

Spark's fiction treats nothing created by man, or woman, as entirely sacred. Her satirical scepticism casts doubt, in her novels, not only on the moral quality of human schemes but on the two things that matter most to her: the private practice of religion and the public art of fiction. As well as commenting on the emptiness of illusions, Spark regularly ridicules believers and exposes as fraudulent the realistic foundations of fiction. Yet she remains a woman with a religious creed and a genuine faith in art. There is, her novels show, a creative world of difference between false faiths and spiritual aspirations, between criminal plots and fictive ploys. Art is, by its aesthetic energy, affirmative. The truth Spark seeks to convey, by an elaborate literary strategy, is a complex one best expressed paradoxically. Individuals, so the cumulative evidence of her fiction implies, exercise their freedom of choice by opting for the idea that most comfortably constrains them; each person chooses the mental chains that link him, or her, to the likeminded, who may turn out to be temperamentally intolerable. As a wildly imaginative woman Spark has found the theological certainties of Roman Catholicism both attractive and agonizing; as a poet by inclination she has discovered in the flexibility of fictional prose a discipline and a dilemma. Her vision focuses most easily on the absurdity of the human condition and she is perfectly serious in treating the spiritual isolation of the individual as a suitable subject for comedy. In fact such a series of contradictions would indicate inconsistency; in Spark's fiction the complexities cohere.

119

NOTES

1 Derek Stanford, *Muriel Spark: A Biographical and Critical Study* (London: Centaur Press, 1963), p. 31.
2 Muriel Spark, 'What Images Return', in Karl Miller (ed.), *Memoirs of a Modern Scotland* (London: Faber & Faber, 1970), p. 152.
3 The main source of stories about Spark's private life is Derek Stanford, *Inside the Forties: Literary Memoirs 1937–1957* (London: Sidgwick & Jackson, 1977). However, Spark, in a letter of 18 March 1986 to Alan Bold, writes 'All Derek Stanford's writings on me range from distorted to sheer invention'.
4 Stanford, 1977, op. cit., p. 149.
5 Stanford, 1963, op. cit., pp. 21–2.
6 Muriel Spark, *Child of Light* (Hadleigh: Tower Bridge Publications, 1951), p. 4.
7 Muriel Spark, *John Masefield* (London: Peter Nevill, 1953), p. 104.
8 Stanford, 1963, op. cit., p. 92. The French original is printed as epigraph to 'The Ballad of the Fanfarlo'.
9 Stanford, 1977, op. cit., p. 189. Stanford mentions hallucinations involving T. S. Eliot but see Spark's remark in note 3.
10 Ibid., pp. 193–5.
11 Muriel Spark, Interview with Malcolm Muggeridge, Granada Television, 2 June 1961.
12 Stefan Kanfer, 'Job Hunting in the Eternal City', *Time*, 16 July 1984.
13 Evelyn Waugh, 'Something Fresh', *Spectator*, 22 February 1957, p. 256.
14 Muriel Spark, *Doctors of Philosophy* (London: Macmillan, 1963), p. 48.
15 Ibid., p. 63.
16 Ibid., p. 31.
17 Muriel Spark, Interview with Philip Toynbee, *Observer Colour Supplement*, 7 November 1971, p. 73.
18 Patricia Stubbs, *Muriel Spark* (Harlow: Longman for the British

Council, 1973), p. 33. 'No one could argue that Muriel Spark is a major novelist. . . .'

19 Kenneth McLeish, *The Penguin Companion to the Arts in the Twentieth Century* (Harmondsworth: Penguin, 1985), p. 181.
20 Spark, 'What Images Return', p. 153.
21 Muriel Spark, Letter of 22 April 1979 to Alan Bold.
22 Spark, *Child of Light*, p. 20.
23 Muriel Spark, 'My Conversion', *Twentieth Century*, Autumn 1961, p. 62.
24 Mark Amory (ed.), *The Letters of Evelyn Waugh* (1980; repr. Harmondsworth: Penguin, 1982), pp. 477–8.
25 Edmund Wilson, *The Triple Thinkers* (1952; repr. Harmondsworth: Pelican, 1962), pp. 28–39.
26 Muriel Spark, Interview with Ian Gillham, 'Writers of Today No. 4', BBC World Service, abridged as 'Keeping It Short', *Listener*, 24 September 1970, pp. 411–13.
27 Muriel Spark, 'The Desegregation of Art', The Blashfield Foundation Address, *Proceedings of the American Academy of Arts and Letters 1971*, p. 24.
28 *The Scotsman*, 18 February 1986, p. 2.
29 Spark, *John Masefield*, p. 174.
30 Frank Kermode, 'The House of Fiction', *Partisan Review*, Spring 1963, repr. in Malcolm Bradbury (ed.), *The Novel Today: Contemporary Writers on Modern Fiction* (London: Fontana, 1977), p. 132.
31 Ibid., p. 133.
32 Amory, op. cit., p. 477.
33 Ibid., p. 478.
34 Biographical note in John Pudney (ed.), *Pick of Today's Short Stories No. 4* (New York: Putnam, 1953).
35 Stanford, 1963, op. cit., p. 61.
36 Amory, op. cit., p. 494.
37 Spark, Interview with Malcolm Muggeridge.
38 Stanford, 1963, op. cit., p. 33. 'In Muriel Spark's first novel, *The Comforters*, there is a free imaginative portrait of her much-loved grandmother in the figure of Louisa Jepp. . . . Mrs Jepp is one of the few characters whom the author seems to love.'
39 E. H. Gombrich, *Meditations on a Hobby Horse* (London: Phaidon Press, 1963), p. 99.
40 Carol B. Ohmann, 'Muriel Spark's *Robinson*', *Critique*, Fall 1965, pp. 70–84.
41 Ruth Whittaker, *The Faith and Fiction of Muriel Spark* (London: Macmillan, 1982), pp. 28–9.
42 Stanford, 1963, op. cit., p. 128.
43 James Hogg, *The Private Memoirs and Confessions of a Justified Sinner* (1824; repr. Harmondsworth: Penguin, 1983), p. 132.

121

44 Quotations from *The Waste Land* in this paragraph occur in 'The Fire Sermon', the third section of the sequence. See T. S. Eliot, *Collected Poems 1909–1962* (London: Faber & Faber, 1963), pp. 71–2.

45 Ibid., p. 68.

46 Stubbs, op. cit., p. 15.

47 According to Ruth Whittaker, op. cit., p. 32.

48 Stanford, 1977, op. cit., p. 184.

49 Muriel Spark, Letter of 5 October 1982 to Alan Bold.

50 Muriel Spark, Letter of 17 February 1983 to Alan Bold.

51 For a consideration of the relationship between actual characters and their fictional counterparts see Alan Bold and Robert Giddings, *Who Was Really Who in Fiction* (Harlow: Longman, 1986). The originals of Holmes and Smiley are identified as Dr Joseph Bell and Dr V. H. H. Green respectively. The most obvious of Spark's originals (Richard Nixon, the prototype of Alexandra in *The Abbess of Crewe*) is discussed.

52 Kermode, op. cit., p. 133.

53 Spark, Interview with Malcolm Muggeridge.

54 Spark, Interview with Ian Gillham.

55 Ibid.

56 Allan Massie, *Muriel Spark* (Edinburgh: Ramsay Head Press, 1979), p. 70.

57 Whittaker, op. cit., p. 34.

58 Spark, *Child of Light*, p. 128.

59 Ibid., p. 133.

60 John Updike, 'Topnotch Witcheries', *New Yorker*, 6 January 1975, p. 76.

61 H. R. Haldeman, *The Ends of Power* (1978; repr. London: Star, 1978), p. 343.

62 Spark, Interview with Malcolm Muggeridge.

63 Biographical note in Pudney, op. cit.

64 Muriel Spark, 'The Mystery of Job's Suffering', *Church of England Newspaper*, 15 April 1955, p. 7.

65 Quoted in Kanfer, op. cit.

BIBLIOGRAPHY

WORKS BY MURIEL SPARK

Verse

The Fanfarlo and Other Verse. Aldington: The Hand and Flower Press, 1952.
Collected Poems 1. London: Macmillan, 1967. New York: Alfred A. Knopf, 1968.
Going Up To Sotheby's and Other Poems. St Albans: Granada, 1982.

Novels

The Comforters. London: Macmillan, 1957. Philadelphia, Pa: J. B. Lippincott, 1957. Paperback: Harmondsworth: Penguin, 1963. New York: Avon, 1964. New York: Perigee, 1984.
Robinson. London: Macmillan, 1958. Philadelphia, Pa: J. B. Lippincott, 1958. Paperback: Harmondsworth: Penguin, 1964. New York: Avon, 1964.
Memento Mori. London: Macmillan, 1959. Philadelphia, Pa: J. B. Lippincott, 1959. New York: Modern Library, 1966 (with *The Ballad of Peckham Rye*). Paperback: Harmondsworth: Penguin, 1961. New York: Meridian Books, 1960. New York: Avon, 1966. New York: Perigee, 1982.
The Ballad of Peckham Rye. London: Macmillan, 1960. Philadelphia, Pa: J. B. Lippincott, 1960. New York: Modern Library, 1966 (with *Memento Mori*). Paperback: Harmondsworth: Penguin, 1963. New York: Dell, 1964. New York: Perigee, 1982.
The Bachelors. London: Macmillan, 1960. Philadelphia, Pa: J. B. Lippincott, 1961. Paperback: Harmondsworth: Penguin, 1963. New York: Dell, 1964. New York: Perigee, 1982.
The Prime of Miss Jean Brodie. First published in the *New Yorker*, 14

October 1961. London: Macmillan, 1961. Philadelphia, Pa: J. B. Lippincott, 1962. Paperback: Harmondsworth: Penguin, 1965. New York: Dell, 1964. New York: New American Library, 1985.

A Muriel Spark Trio. Philadelphia, Pa: J. B. Lippincott, 1962. (Contains *The Comforters*, *Memento Mori* and *The Ballad of Peckham Rye*.)

The Girls of Slender Means. London: Macmillan, 1963. New York: Alfred A. Knopf, 1963. Paperback: Harmondsworth: Penguin, 1966. New York: Avon, 1964. New York: Perigee, 1982.

The Mandelbaum Gate. First published in the *New Yorker*, 15 May, 10 July, 24 July, 7 August 1965. London: Macmillan, 1965. New York: Alfred A. Knopf, 1965. Paperback: Harmondsworth: Penguin, 1967. New York: Fawcett, 1967.

The Public Image. London: Macmillan, 1968. New York: Alfred A. Knopf, 1968. Paperback: Harmondsworth: Penguin, 1970. New York: Ballantine, 1969.

The Driver's Seat. First published in the *New Yorker*, 16 May 1970. London: Macmillan, 1970. New York: Alfred A. Knopf, 1970. Paperback: Harmondsworth: Penguin, 1974. New York: Bantam, 1975. New York: Perigee, 1984.

Not to Disturb. London: Macmillan, 1971. New York: Viking Press, 1972. Paperback: Harmondsworth: Penguin, 1974. New York: Penguin, 1977.

The Hothouse by the East River. London: Macmillan, 1973. New York: Viking Press, 1973. Paperback: Harmondsworth: Penguin, 1975. New York: Penguin, 1977. St Albans: Granada, 1982.

The Abbess of Crewe. London: Macmillan, 1974. New York: Viking Press, 1974. Paperback: Harmondsworth: Penguin, 1975. New York: Penguin, 1978. St Albans: Granada, 1984. New York: Perigee, 1984.

The Takeover. London: Macmillan, 1976. New York: Viking Press, 1976. Paperback: Harmondsworth and New York: Penguin, 1978. St Albans: Granada, 1985.

Territorial Rights. London: Macmillan, 1979. New York: Coward, McCann & Geoghegan, 1979. Paperback: St Albans: Panther, 1980. New York: Perigee, 1984.

Loitering with Intent. London: The Bodley Head, 1981. New York: Coward, McCann & Geoghegan, 1981. Paperback: St Albans: Triad/ Granada, 1982. New York: Perigee, 1982.

The Only Problem. London: The Bodley Head, 1984. New York: Putnam, 1984. Paperback: St Albans: Granada, 1986. New York: Perigee, 1985.

Short stories

The Go-Away Bird and Other Stories. London: Macmillan, 1958. Philadelphia, Pa: J. B. Lippincott, 1960. Paperback: Harmondsworth: Penguin, 1963. Philadelphia, Pa: Lippincott Keystone, 1961.

Voices at Play. London: Macmillan, 1961. Philadelphia, Pa: J. B. Lippincott, 1961. (Contains stories and radio plays written for the BBC Third Programme.)

Collected Stories 1. London: Macmillan, 1967. New York: Alfred A. Knopf, 1968.

Bang-Bang You're Dead and Other Stories. St Albans: Granada, 1982. (Contains stories from *Voices at Play*, 'The First Year of My Life' and 'The Gentile Jewesses'.)

The Stories of Muriel Spark. New York: E. P. Dutton, 1985. (Contains *Collected Stories 1*, 'The First Year of My Life', 'The Gentile Jewesses', 'The Executor', 'The Fortune Teller', 'The Dragon' and 'Another Pair of Hands'.)

For children

The Very Fine Clock. London: Macmillan, 1969. New York: Alfred A. Knopf, 1968.

Play

Doctors of Philosophy. London: Macmillan, 1963. New York: Alfred A. Knopf, 1966. (First performed at the New Arts Theatre Club, London, 2 October 1962.)

Criticism

Tribute to Wordsworth: A Miscellany of Opinion for the Centenary of the Poet's Death (edited with Derek Stanford). London: Wingate, 1950.

Child of Light: A Reassessment of Mary Wollstonecraft Shelley. Hadleigh: Tower Bridge Publications, 1951.

A Selection of Poems by Emily Brontë (edited with an Introduction). London: Grey Walls Press, 1952.

The Brontë Letters (edited with an Introduction). London: Peter Nevill, 1953. Norman, Okla: University of Oklahoma Press, 1954. Repr. London: Macmillan, 1966.

Emily Brontë: Her Life and Work (edited with Derek Stanford). London: Peter Owen, 1953. New York: Coward McCann, 1966. Paperback: London: Hutchinson Arena, 1985.

My Best Mary: Selected Letters of Mary Shelley (edited with Derek Stanford). London: Wingate, 1953.

John Masefield. London: Peter Nevill, 1953. Repr. London: Macmillan, 1962.

Letters of John Henry Newman (edited with Derek Stanford). London: Peter Owen, 1957.

Articles

Poetry Review. Editorials in vol. 38, no. 6, and vol. 39, nos 1–5 (December 1947 to December 1948/January 1949). A leaflet was issued with vol. 39, no. 5, announcing the end of Muriel Spark's editorship.

Forum. Editorial in vol. 1, no. 1 (Summer 1949); Introduction (with Derek Stanford) in vol. 1, no. 2 (undated).

'The Poetry of Anne Brontë'. *New English Weekly*, 26 May 1949.

'The Poet in Mr Eliot's Ideal State'. *Outposts*, 14 (Summer 1949).

'The Dramatic Works of T. S. Eliot'. *Women's Review*, 5 (1949).

'Mary Shelley: A Prophetic Novelist'. *Listener*, 22 February 1951.

'The Religion of an Agnostic: a Sacramental View of the World in the Writings of Proust'. *Church of England Newspaper*, 27 November 1953.

'The Mystery of Job's Suffering'. *Church of England Newspaper*, 15 April 1955.

'How I Became a Novelist'. *John O'London's Weekly*, 3, 61 (1 December 1960).

'My Conversion'. *Twentieth Century* (Autumn 1961).

'The Brontës as Teachers'. *New Yorker*, 22 January 1966.

'What Images Return'. In Karl Miller (ed.), *Memoirs of a Modern Scotland*. London: Faber & Faber, 1970.

'The Desegregation of Art'. The Blashfield Foundation Address, *Proceedings of the American Academy of Arts and Letters 1971*.

Interviews

With Malcolm Muggeridge. 'Appointment with . . .', Granada Television, 2 June 1961.

With Elizabeth Jane Howard. 'Writers in the Present Tense', *Queen*, August 1961.

With Joyce Emerson. 'The Mental Squint of Muriel Spark', *Sunday Times*, 30 September 1962.

With Frank Kermode. 'The House of Fiction: Interviews with Seven English Novelists', *Partisan Review*, Spring 1963. Repr. in Malcolm Bradbury (ed.), *The Novel Today: Contemporary Writers on Modern Fiction*. London: Fontana, 1977.

With Mary Holland. 'The Prime of Muriel Spark', *Observer Colour Supplement*, 17 October 1965.

With George Armstrong. *Guardian*, 30 September 1970.

With Ian Gillham. 'Writers of Today No. 4', BBC World Service, abridged as 'Keeping It Short', *Listener*, 24 September 1970.

With Philip Toynbee. *Observer Colour Supplement*, 7 November 1971.

With Graham Lord. 'The Love Letters that Muriel Spark Refused to Buy', *Sunday Express*, 4 May 1973.

On *Kaleidoscope*. BBC Radio 4, abridged as 'Bugs and Mybug', *Listener*, 28 November 1974.
With Alex Hamilton. *Guardian*, 8 November 1974.
With Lorna Sage. 'The Prime of Muriel Spark', *Observer*, 30 May 1976.

SELECTED CRITICISM OF MURIEL SPARK

Books

Bold, Alan (ed.). *Muriel Spark: An Odd Capacity for Vision*. London: Vision Press, 1984. Totowa, NJ: Barnes & Noble, 1984.

Kemp, Peter. *Muriel Spark*. London: Paul Elek, 1974.

Malkoff, Karl. *Muriel Spark*. New York and London: Columbia University Press, 1968.

Massie, Allan. *Muriel Spark*. Edinburgh: Ramsay Head Press, 1979.

Stanford, Derek. *Muriel Spark: A Biographical and Critical Study*. London: Centaur Press, 1963.

——*Inside the Forties: Literary Memoirs 1937–1957*. London: Sidgwick & Jackson, 1977.

Stubbs, Patricia. *Muriel Spark*. Harlow: Longman for the British Council, 1973.

Whittaker, Ruth. *The Faith and Fiction of Muriel Spark*. London: Macmillan, 1982.

Essays and articles

Bradbury, Malcolm. 'Dark Spark'. *New Society*, 24 September 1970.

——'Muriel Spark's Fingernails'. In *Possibilities: Essays on the State of the Novel*, pp. 247–55. London: Oxford University Press, 1973.

Burgess, Anthony. *Ninety-Nine Novels*. London: Allison & Busby, 1984. (Subtitled 'The Best in English since 1939' it includes brief appreciations of *The Girls of Slender Means*, p. 88, and *The Mandelbaum Gate*, p. 95.)

——*Homage To Qwert Yuiop*. London: Hutchinson, 1986. (Reviews *The Only Problem*, pp. 516–18.)

Hart, Francis Russell. *The Scottish Novel*. London: John Murray, 1978. (Discusses the moral ethos of Spark's fiction, pp. 294–310.)

Hynes, Samuel. 'The Prime of Muriel Spark'. *Commonweal*, 23 February 1962.

Kanfer, Stefan. 'Job Hunting in the Eternal City'. *Time*, 16 July 1984. (Reviews *The Only Problem* with biographical asides.)

Kermode, Frank. *Modern Essays*. London: Fontana, 1971. (Reviews Spark's fiction up to *The Public Image*, pp. 267–83.)

Lodge, David. *The Novelist at the Crossroads*. London: Routledge & Kegan Paul, 1971. (Discusses 'method and meaning' in *The Prime of Miss Jean Brodie*, pp. 119–44.)

Mayne, Richard. 'Fiery Particle: On Muriel Spark'. *Encounter*, 6 December 1965.

Murphy, Carol. 'A Spark of the Supernatural'. *Approach* (Summer 1966).

Murray, Isabel, and Tait, Robert. *Ten Modern Scottish Novels*. Aberdeen: Aberdeen University Press, 1984. (Discusses *The Prime of Miss Jean Brodie*, pp. 100–22.)

Ohmann, Carol B. 'Muriel Spark's *Robinson*'. *Critique* (Fall 1965).

Stanford, Derek. 'The Early Days of Miss Muriel Spark'. *Critic*, 20, 5 (April–May 1962).

——'The Work of Muriel Spark: An Essay on her Fictional Method'. *Month* (August 1962).

Updike, John. 'Topnotch Witcheries'. *New Yorker*, 6 January 1975. (Reviews *The Abbess of Crewe*.)

Waugh, Evelyn. 'Something Fresh'. *Spectator*, 22 February 1957. (Reviews *The Comforters*.)

——'Threatened Genius: Difficult Saint'. *Spectator*, 7 July 1961. (Reviews *The Bachelors*.)

Wilson, Angus. 'Journey to Jerusalem'. *Observer*, 17 October 1965.